T0357245

GOLF
STROKE BY STROKE

BRIAN CROWELL

Publisher Mike Sanders
Art & Design Director William Thomas
Editorial Director Ann Barton
Proofreader Georgette Beatty
Layout Ayanna Lacey

Updated and reprinted from *Idiot's Guide's: Golf* © 2014
Published in the United States by DK Publishing
1745 Broadway, 20th Floor, New York, NY 10019

The authorized representative in the EEA is Dorling Kindersley Verlag GmbH.
Arnulfstr. 124, 80636 Munich, Germany

Copyright © 2025 Penguin Random House LLC
DK, a Division of Penguin Random House LLC
25 26 27 28 29   10 9 8 7 6 5 4 3 2 1
001-348308-MAY2025

A catalog record for this book
is available from the Library of Congress.
ISBN 978-0-59396-505-4

DK books are available at special discounts when purchased
in bulk for sales promotions, premiums, fund-raising, or educational use. For details,
contact SpecialSales@dk.com

Printed and bound in China

Photos by Stephen Szurlej, with the following exceptions
p. 229 Gerard Brown © Dorling Kindersley
p. 250 Alex Havret © Dorling Kindersley

www.dk.com

MIX
Paper | Supporting
responsible forestry
FSC™ C018179

This book was made with Forest
Stewardship Council™ certified
paper – one small step in DK's
commitment to a sustainable future.
Learn more at
www.dk.com/uk/information/sustainability

Contents

introduction

Welcome to the world of golf! I first want to thank you for taking this important step toward learning and understanding this great game. I'm delighted to have this opportunity to introduce you to a sport that has so much to offer. I've been fortunate to teach golf and help my students discover the many rewards of this wonderful sport. It's a thrill to help them hit that first great shot, and to assist them as they continue to improve and enjoy the game. But authoring this book has taken my involvement to another level entirely. It's an honor to introduce golf to such a limitless audience. And with that honor comes the responsibility to make this book very easy to understand, very effective, and very entertaining.

I've spent decades as a PGA professional, studying and gathering knowledge of the swing, learning nuances of the game, and designing improvement programs for my students. I know firsthand how much golf instruction information is available. There are countless videos, magazine articles, and instructional television programs. It can seem as if every golf broadcaster, instructor, or golf buddy you hear from has a different theory on the golf swing. It can be confusing and a bit overwhelming for a beginner who wants to try golf for the first time. And that's *exactly* why I've written the book that is now in your hands!

Golf Stroke by Stroke is an intelligent approach to learning and understanding the game. My goal is clear: to provide you with a simple, step-by-step guide for learning the golf swing, and to give you the additional information necessary to feel comfortable in a golf setting. As a bonus, there are chapters dedicated to golf fitness, playing opportunities, practice drills designed to further your improvement, and more.

I'm very pleased to provide this essential resource for the aspiring golfer. You're entering an exciting world, and there are so many directions you can take with this sport. Golf can be relaxing, golf can be competitive, and golf will provide you with enjoyable challenges and camaraderie. This game promotes health and fitness, celebrates the environment, and can take you to some of the most beautiful destinations on the planet. Golf can be enjoyed as a single, or with family, friends, business associates, or the other fellow golfers you meet at the course. As you can tell, golf has had a powerful and positive impact on my life, and I'm excited to share the benefits and help introduce this sport to you and so many others.

This is a game you can play for the rest of your life. So enjoy this book, and enjoy your journey with golf!

a word to the lefties

A quick note to readers who play golf "from the other side of the ball": To keep this book as simple as possible, I've written from the perspective of a right-handed golfer. My apologies to the left-handers, but please understand that the content in this book is just as valuable to you. Many left-handers naturally transpose instructions to the other side, but if you are new to golf or don't have experience switching instructions to a leftie point of view, please "flip" my instructions accordingly. The beautiful photos in this book can be relevant to you as well—just hold the book up to a mirror ... seriously!

acknowledgments

I'm certainly very proud of what has been accomplished with this book, which required the hard work and long hours of an excellent team. I want to thank Alpha Books for this opportunity, and Karyn Gerhard, John Etchison, and Becky Batchelor for their expertise in orchestrating, editing, and designing this beautiful book. Thanks also to my agent, Marilyn Allen, and to Lorin Anderson for thinking of me for this project. This book relies on powerful images, and I could not have told the story without the incredible work of one of the best photographers in the golf biz, Steve Szurlej.

Steve's photography is even more powerful thanks to the beautiful backdrop of GlenArbor Golf Club in Bedford Hills, New York. Thanks to the members and owners of GlenArbor for the use of your facility and for supporting me in this endeavor. Thanks, too, to the GlenArbor professional staff, Rob, Debbie, Dave, Jesse, and Ellen, who covered for me during my absences. I also appreciate the support of TaylorMade, Adidas, and reps RJ and Reva for outfitting me with the best in equipment and apparel. Thanks also to Mike Zisman and Billy Condon of Golf Genius Software, Tommie Copper, and Mark Jeffers. Thank you PGA of America, the Metropolitan Section, and my fellow PGA professionals who do an incredible job of teaching, growing, and promoting the game of golf.

Finally, and most importantly, I want to thank my family. I'm so lucky to have parents who gave me so many options and continue to give me advice and encouragement. My grandparents built my first golf course—with coffee cans sunk in the ground around their house. Years later, they gave me a junior membership to Osiris Country Club, where I truly got hooked on the game. And my ultimate inspiration comes from my incredible wife, Wendy, and our three amazing children, Kevin, Casey, and Christina. Thank you for your love, support, and understanding of my unique work schedule. The four of you give me such incredible joy and perspective, and truly make every day special.

getting started

golf jargon: a primer

Like most sports, golf has its own language. Although I've written this book with the beginner golfer in mind, you will find some general golf terms used in the instructions. These are the terms you'll hear around the course, or from any instructor, and are important to understand when learning the game. You may have heard these words before, but in golf they sometimes have a slightly different meaning. I've put together this primer of the golf terms to help you start learning the lingo. Don't worry, though—you don't need to memorize these before you start learning to swing the club! Later on we'll look at some interesting golf slang and "insider lingo," but for now, here are some basic terms.

address   The position a golfer gets into as he prepares to make a swing.

alignment   Refers to positions prior to the swing. If your feet, knees, hips, shoulders, and forearms are parallel with your intended target line, you have addressed the ball with proper alignment.

approach   A golf shot that is expected to reach the green.

axis   Refers to the spine, which is the center of the swing motion, or the axis the body swings around.

back foot   The foot that is farthest from the target.

back nine   Usually refers to holes numbered 10 through 18, or the second nine holes of a complete 18-hole round. If players happen to start on hole number 10, then holes 1 through 9 would actually be their back nine, or the second nine holes played.

backswing   The first part of the golf swing, where the club is moving back away from the ball. The backswing is completed when the club changes direction, and begins to move back toward the ball.

balance   A stable finish to a golf swing. A good golfer finishes their swings in balance.

baseball grip
A grip style where all eight fingers are in contact with the club. Similar to the grip used on a baseball bat.

birdie   A score of one less than the assigned par for a given hole. If par is 4, and you get the ball in the cup in 3 strokes, you scored a birdie.

bogey   A score of one more than the assigned par for a given hole. If par is 4, and it takes you 5 strokes to get the ball in the hole, you scored a bogey.

break   The curving path a golf ball is expected to take when it is rolled on uneven ground. Undulations in the surface of the putting green can cause the ball to break in different directions.

bunker   A huge hole in the ground that is filled with sand. Bunkers are designed to capture errant shots. They are frequently found near the putting green. Those guarding the fairway landing zones are called "fairway bunkers."

caddie   A person who carries a player's clubs during a round of golf. They also assist the player and offer advice when appropriate.

chip   A low shot that travels farther on the ground than it does in the air. The chip is made with a smaller swing motion and is frequently used to get a ball onto the putting surface from only a short distance away.

choke   When a player performs much worse than expected, or does not perform well under pressure.

choke down   To position your hands farther down the grip toward the clubhead, effectively making the club shorter.

closed clubface   When the clubface is aiming left of the intended target line, it's closed (for a right-hander). A ball struck with a closed clubface is likely to go left.

closed stance   When a right-handed player's feet are aligned to the right of the intended target line, that player has a closed stance.

clubface   The front, flat portion of the club that is designed to contact the ball.

clubhead   The end portion of a golf club that is designed to hit the ball. It is connected to the club shaft by the hosel or neck of the club.

cupped wrist   A position easily noticed at the top of a player's backswing where the left wrist is supinated or bent so that the back of the left hand is higher than the left forearm.

divot   A piece of turf that has been torn from the ground by a golf swing. A divot can also refer to the hole in the ground that is left after a divot has been taken.

double bogey   A score that is 2 strokes higher than the given par of a hole. If par is 3, and it takes you 5 strokes to complete the hole, you scored a double bogey.

double eagle   A score that is 3 strokes below par on a given hole. If it takes you only 2 strokes to complete a par-5 hole, you scored a double eagle. (Yes, the double eagle is *very* rare.)

downswing   The portion of the swing that moves downward from the top of the backswing toward the ball.

draw   A term to describe the flight of a ball. When a right-handed player strikes a ball and it launches slightly to the right of the target line, and then curves back gently to the left toward the target, that flight defines a draw.

driver   The club that has the least amount of loft (other than the putter). This club is also the longest club in the bag and is expected to hit the ball the farthest. It's normally used to hit a ball off a tee on longer holes.

eagle   A score of 2 below par on a given hole. If you're playing a par-5 hole and only need 3 shots to get the ball in the cup, you scored an eagle.

fade   A term used to describe the flight of a ball. When a right-handed player strikes a ball and it launches slightly to the left of the target line and drifts back gently to the right toward the target, the player has hit a fade.

fairway   Closely mown grass that defines the ideal landing zone on a par-4 or par-5 hole. This shorter grass is a very desirable target. If you hit the fairway, your next shot will be easier.

fairway wood   Similar in shape but slightly smaller than the driver. This club has more loft than the driver and can hit the ball a long way from the fairway or from the tee.

fat shot   When the club accidentally hits the ground before striking the ball. The turf then gets stuck between the clubface and the ball, preventing the ball from flying as far as it normally would.

flat swing   A flat swing occurs when the club travels on a relatively horizontal path. In an amusement park analogy, a flat swing moves more like a merry-go-round than a Ferris wheel.

follow-through   The portion of the swing that takes place after the ball has been struck. The follow-through leads you to the finish of your swing.

Fore!   A shouted warning on the golf course that is yelled loudly when a ball is likely to hit someone.

front foot   The foot that is closer to the target.

front nine   Generally defined as hole numbers 1 through 9, or the first nine holes played out of an 18-hole round.

grain (grass)   The grain refers to the direction that the blades of grass are growing in. You can putt "with" the grain (grass is growing away from you), or "against" the grain (grass is growing toward you).

grip   The position your hands form as they hold the golf club. Also refers to the actual part of the club that a player holds while swinging.

handicap   A number that helps measure the skill level of a player. A higher handicap number means that golfer is likely to shoot a higher score. A handicap generally gives an expectation of how that player should perform.

hazard   An area of the course that should be avoided. Hazards can come in the form of water or sand bunkers, and they are expected to challenge or penalize a player for a poor shot.

heel   The portion of the clubhead that is closest to the shaft and hosel.

hook   Describes the flight pattern of a golf ball. When a ball is struck by a right-handed player and it spins and curves dramatically to the left, it's called a hook.

hosel   The elongated portion of the clubhead that connects it to the shaft. Also known as the neck of the club.

hybrid club   A golf club that is a cross between an iron and a fairway wood. It actually looks like a smaller version of a fairway wood, but is designed to replace your long irons.

impact   That critical moment in the swing when your golf club makes contact with the ball.

irons   The clubs other than the driver, fairway woods, hybrids, or putter are referred to as irons. The clubhead is made of metal, and they are numbered (most sets include numbers 4 through 9 plus wedges).

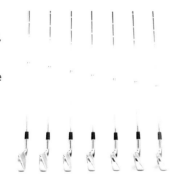

lie   The position of your ball on the ground. If it's sitting nicely on beautiful, level turf, you have a great lie. A ball hidden deep in the rough is in a bad lie.

line   An imaginary path that you would like your ball to travel on.

links   Another term for golf course. "Links" specifically refers to courses that have no trees and are located near large bodies of water. Links courses are very popular in Europe.

loft   The angle of the clubface relative to the ground. Loft is measured in degrees. The greater the loft, the higher and shorter a ball will travel.

open clubface   For a right-handed player, an open clubface will point to the right of the intended target line. A ball struck with an open clubface is likely to miss the target to the right.

open stance   If a player sets up and a line drawn across his feet is aligned to the left of the target, he has an open stance.

par   The number of strokes that an accomplished player should require to complete a given hole. The par score for a hole is determined by the length and difficulty of the hole.

Brian	0			PAR			WHITE
				5			491
				4			356
				3			144
				4			393
				5			471
				4			341

pulled shot   A pulled shot is a shot that is accidentally launched to the left of the intended target (for a right-handed player).

push   A push is a shot that (for a right-handed player) accidentally launches to the right of the intended target line.

putt   A stroke made with a putter. A putt typically takes place on a putting green, but a putt can also be taken from just off the green.

reading the green   The process of determining how a ball will roll, and which way it might curve after being struck on the putting surface.

release   A term that describes the natural closing of the clubface through and just after impact with the ball. An effective release will allow the club to swing past the hands after impact, then on to a comfortable finish.

rough   Higher, thicker grass that surrounds the tee boxes, fairways, and greens.

sand trap   Another term for a sand bunker. Bunker is the preferred term.

scramble   A format of the game where all players in a group hit a drive, and after choosing the best drive of the group, the players all play their second shots from that spot. They then choose the best of the second shots and all play from that spot. This continues until the ball is holed. (For more detail, see Chapter 15.) A great format for beginners!

setup   A specified system or arrangement. In golf, setup usually refers to a player's pre-shot address position.

shaft   The long cylindrical part of the golf club that connects the clubhead to the grip, usually made of either steel or graphite.

short game   A general term that describes all shots taken from 100 yards (91m) or closer to the green. Short game includes putting, chipping, pitching, bunker play, and most wedge shots.

slice   A shot that spins dramatically and curves far to the right (for a right-hander) in the air, and usually misses the target to the right. Sometimes referred to as a "banana."

slope   A gradual incline. Also the term for a slope rating, or a number that represents the difficulty of a golf course. The higher the slope number, the more difficult the course.

sole   The bottom of the clubhead. The sole of the club rests on the ground during the address position.

splash shot   A term I use to describe a successful bunker shot. This shot "splashes" sand out of the bunker, as opposed to digging down steeply. When you splash sand, you are using the sand wedge effectively. A ball that rests on the sand will be blasted out and onto the green nicely with a splash shot.

stance   A word to describe your address position. The position you take just before making a golf swing.

stroke   The forward motion of a golf club when there is intent to strike a ball.

stroke play   A very common format of play, also known as medal play, where each stroke during the course of an 18-hole round is totaled for a player's score.

sweet spot   The very center of the clubface, and the ideal spot to make contact with the ball.

swing   In golf, a swing is a motion made with a golf club. The motion is designed to deliver the clubhead to a ball, and launch the ball toward a target.

takeaway   The first part of the backswing.

tee box   The first swing for each hole on the golf course is made from a tee box. This is the level, closely mown area where the ball is first teed up. Courses  often feature multiple tee boxes for each hole. The (usually colored) tee markers that further define your first starting position are located on the tee box.

tempo   Refers to the speed and rhythm with which you swing the club.

thin shot   When the leading edge of the clubface strikes the golf ball near its equator. A thin shot will generally fly much lower and farther than normal, with virtually no spin.

trajectory   This word describes the flight of a golf ball, or the curving shape of that flight path.

wedge   One of several of the most lofted golf clubs. Included in the wedge family are the pitching wedge (PW), sand wedge (SW), and lob wedge (LW). The wedge launches the ball on a very high trajectory, and is designed to land and stop the ball on the putting surface.

the equipment

We live in a world that embraces technology, and product improvements take place at a very rapid rate. Everyone seems to want the latest phone, or this year's new and improved computer. Golfers are inundated with the same temptations. Although you don't need the very latest equipment to enjoy golf, today's technology has certainly made the game a bit easier. But please take note: you *do not* need to run out and purchase a full set of golf clubs just to try the sport or take a lesson. In fact, most PGA instructors have clubs you can use for free during a lesson. And if you go to a driving range, you can borrow or rent clubs. Most courses offer rental sets, so you don't even need your own equipment to play. New equipment can be expensive, so borrowing from a friend or looking for a good used set of clubs might be a wise choice as you learn this great sport.

Whether you buy, rent, or borrow your clubs, it's important to know how and when to use them. In this chapter I will discuss the different components of a club, the various clubs that are available, and when they should be used. You will also learn everything you need to know regarding golf gloves, bags, balls, and even the cart you drive. And finally, I'll help you look the part with advice on golf attire and shoes. This chapter will help prepare you for a complete golf experience.

the clubs

A golfer is allowed to use as many as 14 different clubs during a round of golf. Each of these clubs has a slightly different purpose, and they differ in shape and size. The longer clubs are called **woods** or **metal woods,** and include the longest club in your bag, the driver. These clubs feature a bigger clubhead and less loft or angle built into the clubface. The shorter clubs have greater loft. In contrast to the woods, the shorter **_irons_** will launch the ball higher in the air while covering less distance. Clubs provide different results for different people. The distance expected from a 7-iron, for example, depends on the strength and skill of the player. For a professional, the 7-iron may hit a ball 165 yards (150m); for a beginner, that same club may hit the ball 125 yards (114m). Before heading to the course, it's helpful to figure out the distance each club gives you. Before describing the different club options available, I want to illustrate the various components of a club.

Do I need all of those clubs?

The set of clubs shown here is actually the set I use every day, both to teach and to play. This is a complete set of 14 clubs, but don't worry—you don't need all of these clubs to start off! In fact, a little later in the chapter we'll talk about your starter bag—the basic clubs you should have to start your golf journey.

If you don't want to spend top dollar on your first set of clubs, a good option is to buy used clubs. Of course, it's always good to see the clubs before you buy them, so your best bet is to ask the golf pro at your local course. But if you want to roll the dice, there are also great deals to be found at online auctions.

Anatomy of a Golf Club

Grip: The grip is important because it provides your only contact point with the club. Grips come in varying thicknesses (ladies/juniors, standard, midsize, and oversize) depending on preference and the size of the golfer's hands. Grips also come in a variety of materials, and a wide array of color choices. Grips do wear out over time. If they become too firm or slick, it's recommended you have a new set of grips put on your clubs.

Shaft: The shaft connects the grip to the clubhead. Shafts are made primarily from steel or graphite. Graphite shafts are usually found in drivers, fairway woods, and hybrids, but they can be used in any club. Graphite is usually a touch lighter, and better suited to absorb vibration. Steel shafts are commonly found in irons, wedges, and putters. Shafts are available in different flexes. Players who swing at lower speeds should use a weaker (or more flexible) shaft than players who swing with more power. The most common options for shaft flex are Ladies (L-flex), Seniors (M-flex), Regular (R), Stiff or Firm (S), and extra stiff (X).

Grip

Shaft

Hosel: The hosel or neck connects the clubhead to the shaft. If a player's swing gets off-track, this portion of the club may accidentally strike the ball, resulting in what is known as a "shank" or a "hosel rocket." A shanked shot tends to fly dramatically off to the right or left. Try to avoid striking the ball with the hosel!

Clubhead: This is the business end of the club, and is responsible for meeting the ball during your swing. The clubhead is divided into a number of named sections. The *clubface* is the front side of the club, which makes contact with the ball. It has long parallel grooves that are designed to channel turf and water away from contact with the ball and help to put spin on the ball, which allows a player to control the shot. The perfect center of the clubface is the *sweet spot*—hitting the ball there provides the best results. The outside of the clubhead is known as the *toe* of the club. Inside the sweet spot and closer to the shaft, you'll find the *heel* of the club. When you look down at your club from a typical address position, you'll see what's called the *top line* if you're looking at an iron, or the *crown* if you're looking at a wood. The forward-most edge of a club (closest to the ball at address) is the *leading edge*—the best indicator of where you're aiming the club. The bottom of the clubhead, the part that rests on the ground at address, is called the *sole* of the club.

Hosel

Clubhead

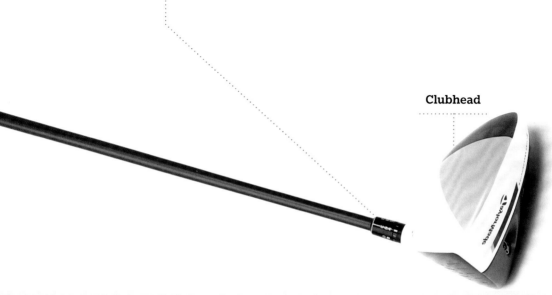

The Driver

The driver is the longest club in the bag, and when swung properly, it will hit the ball the farthest. The driver is usually used on par 5s and long par 4s where you have a lot of yardage to cover. Some players opt to tee off with fairway woods or hybrids on holes with very narrow fairways. But if you are confident and/or faced with a generous landing area, a well-struck driver provides a great advantage. It has the largest clubhead, and it comes in a variety of lofts (angle of the clubface). The most common loft is 10 degrees, but if you hit the ball too high with your driver, you can find lower lofts (9.5, 9, 8.5, etc.). Players with slower swings usually benefit from higher lofts, such as 11 or 12 degrees, and some ladies' drivers come with as much as 15 degrees of loft.

With its large clubface and seeming potential to launch your ball all over the place, you may be afraid to use the driver when you first start out—but don't be! Actually, that large clubface gives the driver the most forgiving hitting area of any club in your bag. Remember also that when you use the driver, your ball is up on a tee, so you're always hitting from level ground. Don't be afraid to pull out the big boy and swing away!

Fairway Woods

Fairway woods look very similar to a driver, but they're shorter, the clubhead is smaller, and they have more loft on the clubface. Although it has been many years since these clubs were made of wood, the name has stuck (although they're sometimes referred to as fairway metals). They are generally associated with a number: 3-wood, 5-wood, 7-wood, etc. The higher the number, the higher and shorter the ball will travel. These clubs can be used from the tee on shorter par 4s, but as their name implies, they're designed to effectively hit the ball long distances from the fairway.

Hybrids

In recent years, hybrid clubs have become very popular. They look a bit like fairway woods, but their heads are smaller and they have more loft. Hybrids have taken the place of longer irons. They're easier to hit, they fly a bit higher, and they travel the same distance as those long irons. They come in a variety of lofts, and frequently have text on their sole that indicates the iron they replace (3h is a hybrid designed to replace a 3-iron). Hybrids are also capable of hitting shots out of lighter rough, which was very difficult to do with long irons.

Wedges

I discussed the pitching wedge as one of your irons, but wedges deserve a section of their own. Wedges come in varying lofts. The pitching wedge has the least amount of loft among the wedges and will hit the ball nearly as far as a 9-iron. The gap wedge has a little more loft than the pitching wedge, followed by the sand wedge and finally the lob wedge, which has the most loft of any club in the bag and will hit the ball the shortest distance. Wedges can be used to hit full shots into greens from close range, and if you happen to miss a green, the wedges are extremely helpful. Since they have a lot of loft, wedges cut through heavy rough and sand and are very effective when escaping difficult course conditions.

Irons

Irons are usually purchased as a set of 7 clubs. An example of an iron set would be 4-, 5-, 6-, 7-, 8-, and 9-irons plus a PW (pitching wedge). 1-, 2-, and 3-irons are much less common these days due to the popularity of hybrids. Irons are used from the tee on shorter par 3s and on any hole for "approach" shots, shots where you expect to reach the green. As you get closer to the green, you will use irons with a higher number (the 8-iron will fly higher and shorter than the 7-iron). Irons differ in length, and the higher the number, the shorter the club. Iron clubheads come in two basic types: forged and cast. Forged clubs are sculpted from a block of solid metal. These clubs have excellent feel when you hit the sweet spot, but they're not very forgiving on off-center hits. Molten metal is poured into a mold to create cast clubs. They have more of a cavity behind the clubface that makes them much more forgiving. While very skilled players often prefer the feel of forged clubheads, most golfers (and certainly beginners) should play with cast irons.

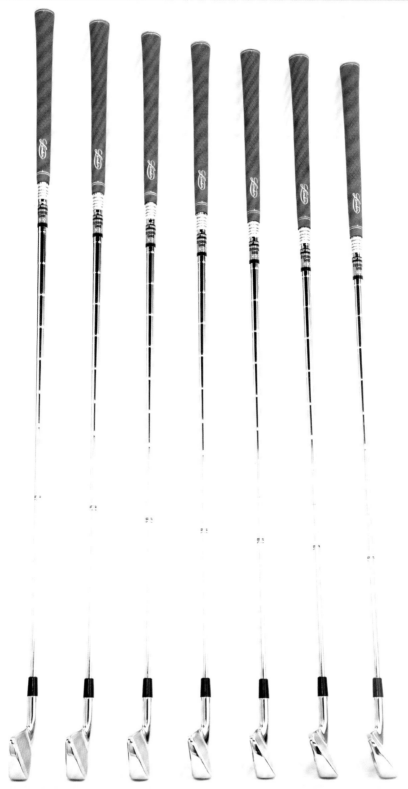

Putters

While they can be used from closely mown turf just off the green, putters are primarily used on the putting surface. Putters come in all shapes, sizes, and lengths. This club is responsible for rolling the ball into the cup to conclude each hole. It's used more than any other club in your bag, yet most players spend far too little time practicing their putting. It's very important to find a putter that works well for you, and you should also like the look of your putter. There are literally thousands of putter head styles, but they can be separated into three general categories: traditional blade is the most common. The half-mallet has more mass behind the sweet spot, and full mallet styles are the largest and frankly the most creative. I would recommend you try a number of different putters before making a purchase.

Putters come in more shapes, styles, and sizes than any other club. The style of putter you choose is really all a matter of preference—test them out to find the one that works best for you. See the three examples on the opposite page.

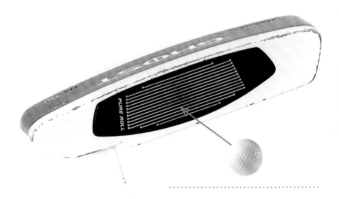

A Soft Touch

The putters on this spread are called "insert" putters—they feature a synthetic material in the middle of the clubface that allows for a softer feel when you putt. Not all putters have these inserts. You may like a more traditional face—it's all about trying them out and seeing what you like best.

Anchoring Putters

Putters are traditionally the shortest club in your bag, but some golfers prefer a longer club to help anchor their swing. There are two types: the "belly putter," named because the grip end of the club is actually anchored in the player's belly, and the "long putter," which is anchored with the player's left hand at the center of their chest. Although the higher anchor points on these clubs help players with their pendulum movement, as of 2016 the anchoring style of putting is no longer considered a legal stroke.

The half-mallet: The half mallet has a little more forgiveness when it comes to off-center hits and allows for easier alignment.

Full mallet head: The full mallet head offers the most in terms of alignment assistance, by keeping the putter face square and perimeter weighted to assist with off-center hits.

Traditional head: Some golfers have a difficult time looking down at the strange heads of the other two, so they go for the traditional putter.

your starter bag

As I mentioned earlier in this chapter, you don't need your own set of clubs to start learning and playing golf. You can borrow clubs or even rent clubs at most golf facilities. But if you decide to buy your own clubs, consider a "starter set." The starter set features regulation equipment, but not the maximum number of 14 clubs. There are no rules that prohibit you from starting with just a partial set—in fact, you could play golf with just one club and a putter if you wanted! The starter set of clubs is obviously more cost-effective than purchasing all 14, and it still provides you with a variety of clubs to play and practice with. I've assembled the set shown in the photo for consideration.

A driver is ideal for use off the tee on longer holes. A hybrid club will give you plenty of length from the fairway and light rough. The 5-, 7-, and 9-irons will provide a nice variety of distances for approach shots. And in case you miss the green, a pitching wedge or sand wedge will allow you to chip, pitch, or even blast from the sand effectively. The putter, of course, is responsible for rolling the ball into the cup. This 7-club set doesn't offer the full-set multitude of different distances, but it certainly provides a comfortable range of shots. A starter set is an adequate and very cost-effective option to consider.

IN THE BAG

As I mentioned earlier, it's a good idea to keep track of the distance each club gives you. Here's a handy place to jot down the distances for each of the clubs in your starter bag—plus a few extra spaces to use if you pick up more clubs.

	CLUB	MY DISTANCE
1	Driver	....
2	Hybrid	....
3	5-Iron	....
4	7-Iron	....
5	9-Iron	....
6	Pitching Wedge	....
7	Sand Wedge	....
8	Putter	N/A
	....	....
	....	....

balls and tees

Every golf ball is constructed to fairly precise specifications. They need to be no less than 1.68" (4.3cm) in diameter and must weigh no greater than 1.62 ounces (46g). However, there are many different dimple patterns, colors, and materials that can be used. The two main categories for golf balls can be described as:

1. **Distance.** These balls have a harder cover that is more difficult to spin. They tend to fly a little farther and a little straighter. Distance balls are cheaper than balls in the second category.

2. **Performance.** These balls have a slightly softer cover, and better players like them because they feel softer off the clubface. Performance balls are easier to spin, and they tend to hold or stay on the greens better. They

are also considerably more expensive. Yes, spin is fun on the greens, but spin can also curve your ball into the woods. Beginning players should save some money and buy the cheaper balls that fly farther and straighter! Golf balls are usually sold by the sleeve (three balls) or by the dozen.

Tees are used to elevate the golf ball prior to contact. The tee can only be used when playing your opening shot on each hole. In other words, you can place your ball on a tee only when playing from the teeing ground of each hole. Tees come in a wide variety of styles, sizes, and colors. They're usually made from wood or plastic. Longer tees are useful when hitting with today's extra-large driver heads, but shorter tees are sufficient when teeing off with fairway woods, hybrids, or irons.

golf bags

The golf bag has one main purpose: to hold your clubs. But golf bags are made with many pockets that hold balls, tees, water bottles, rain gear, an umbrella, etc. Golf bags come in two main categories:

1. **Cart bag.** These bags are much bigger and heavier and are expected to be loaded onto a cart, not carried by a golfer or caddie.

2. **Carry bag.** These bags are lighter and easier to carry. Some feature a double strap (for using both shoulders), and others have only one strap. Many carry bags also have retractable legs, or stands, that will swing out and support the bag and keep it upright after setting it down on the ground.

cart bag

carry bag

attire

For years, golf clothing was a punch line for comedians, but the styles today are very sharp and feature moisture-wicking materials that absorb sweat and make you extra comfortable. Still, you don't need to buy expensive golf outfits your first time out—you will always be safe with a pair of casual dress pants and a collared polo shirt. There are two pieces of attire you may want to consider, however: shoes and gloves.

Shoes

Golf shoes are designed with tread patterns and soft plastic spikes that help to grip the ground and give you better traction during your swings. These golf shoes definitely make you feel more stable, but they're not necessarily required for playing golf. Many golf courses will allow you to play in tennis sneakers or flat-soled shoes, so call ahead to see if golf shoes are necessary.

Gloves

Another piece of equipment you might want to consider is the golf glove. Gloves are made of fine leather or synthetic leather that helps to give you a consistent grip on the club. They come as single gloves in a package, not a pair. A right-handed golfer will wear the glove on his left hand, and the leftie will wear a glove on his right hand. The important thing when choosing a glove is sizing. It should fit your hand snugly and comfortably and act almost like a second layer of skin. A glove is not required, and some players never wear one, but I would recommend using a glove. It assists in giving you comfortable and consistent contact with your clubs. They do wear out quickly if you're playing and practicing a lot, so don't wait too long to replace a slick, torn glove.

And since we're talking about calling ahead, you might want to check on the general dress code before you show up at a golf facility. Many courses will not allow denim, cut-off shorts, tank tops, or t-shirts.

the golf course

In football, the playing field is always 100 yards (91m) in length. A regulation basketball rim is always 10 feet (3m) off the ground. The distance between bases is always 90 feet (27m) in Major League Baseball. But with golf, every course is different. You could travel the world and find the same dimensions for every bowling alley, but no two golf holes are the same. In fact, golf courses come in a very wide variety of styles, and they have a multitude of terrain features, plants, and wildlife.

Golf courses in Canada look very different from golf courses in Florida, and golf courses in China and Scotland each have their own unique characteristics. In North America, "parkland" courses are common. Parkland-style courses have relatively lush, green turf and holes that are frequently lined with trees. In Europe, you are more likely to find "links"-style courses that have firmer, wind-swept turf, deep sharp-edged bunkers, and very few (if any) trees. Links courses were originally built along the sea, with 9 holes constructed out in one direction (like links in a chain) and 9 holes then returning to the clubhouse. Although golf courses are very different from each other, there is one common theme. Throughout the world, golf courses provide some of the most beautiful scenery imaginable. The beauty comes from the natural land that courses are carved from, as well as the high levels of professional maintenance they receive. In this chapter, I'll discuss the different elements of a golf course and various conditions you might find. I'll also explain the different types of golf holes and define differences between golf course styles.

anatomy of a golf course

Tee

A tee is a small wooden or plastic peg that you place a golf ball on for the opening shot on each hole. But "tee" has another meaning. The tee (or teeing ground, or tee box) is the closely mown area from which you begin play on each golf hole. In addition to being closely mown, teeing grounds are perfectly level and also allow you to set your ball on a tee. Therefore, they offer the best conditions for that initial golf shot. Most courses feature multiple teeing grounds for each hole. The more advanced golfers will play from the teeing ground that is farthest from the green. The less experienced golfers (or those who don't hit the ball quite as far) will play from teeing grounds that are closer to the hole. Ladies, seniors, juniors, and beginning golfers will often play from the more forward (or closer) teeing ground.

Golfers with high clubhead speeds tee off here

Golfers with slower speeds tee off here

Tee Markers

Tee actually has a third meaning as well. Placed on the teeing grounds are *tee markers,* or "tees" that further clarify the starting point for each hole. Tee markers come in different colors, and there will always be two markers for each color. An example of varying yardage/difficulty by tee color could be as follows: A hole may be 487 yards (445m) from the black (championship) tee markers, 440 yards (402m) from the blue tees, 407 yards (372m) from the blue/white, 379 yards (346m) from the whites, and 327 yards (299m) from the green (forward) tees. It's important to choose the set of tees that best suits your level of play.

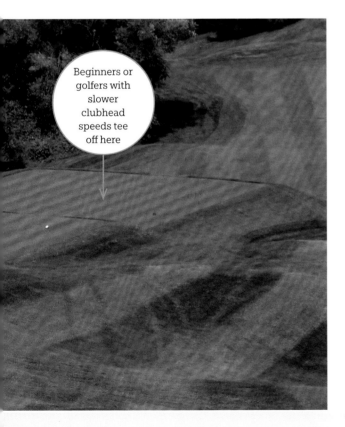

Beginners or golfers with slower clubhead speeds tee off here

Fairway

Like the teeing grounds, fairways are closely mown. The height of the grass is usually identical to that of teeing ground turf, and it is usually the same species of grass. Fairways, however, feature slopes and undulations and stretch from just in front of the teeing ground all the way to the green. If you aim properly and make a nice swing, you will be rewarded with a ball that lands and stays in the "short grass." From the fairway, golfers will have the best chance of hitting their next shot cleanly. Since the grass is cut short, it's relatively easy to make good contact and control the flight of your ball.

Rough

Rough is the deeper, thicker grass located on either side of the fairway and around the green. It's a different species of grass than fairway turf and typically appears darker in color. This grass is longer and much more difficult to play from. Golfers who hit shots off-line and miss fairways and greens will be challenged by the rough. The longer blades of grass are likely to slow down the club as it approaches the ball, and often twist the clubface in different directions. The long grass also gets trapped between the clubhead and the ball, making it difficult to predict shot distances. If escaping this long, thick grass was simple, they would've named it "easy" instead of rough.

The First Cut

The "first cut" is found at the edges of the fairway. This narrow strip is a transition area between the fairway and the rough. It's generally the same type of grass as the rough. Although not as short as fairway turf, the first cut is mown closer than the regular (or primary) rough. If you hit a poor shot, it will usually find the primary rough (or a more penal hazard), but a shot that is just a bit off-line may get lucky enough to stop in the first cut. Shots played from this condition are easier to control than shots from the rough, but a small amount of grass will still get trapped between the clubface and the ball, making it difficult to judge distances accurately.

Many golfers are amazed when they experience the lush green of the fairway for the first time—some even think the grass is synthetic, it's so perfect! It's not synthetic—it's science. Superintendents spend years in training to learn how to cultivate that lush green turf. Golf courses are also mowed and maintained with the finest equipment available. So, don't feel bad that your backyard doesn't look like a fairway!

Rough

The First Cut

Fairway

Green and Fringe

The ultimate destination for your ball is the hole, or the cup. Each flagstick is located in a cup, which is found on the green. The green features a different type of grass, which is usually lighter in color than even the fairway. Grass on the green is cut very short with a special mower, and appears as smooth as carpet. Some courses even use a roller machine to make the turf extra smooth. The green is the designated putting surface for each hole, and the only club you should use on the greens is your putter. You should treat the greens with extra care. Be careful not to scuff your feet, and *never* take a full swing or make a divot on the putting surface. The greens are surrounded by a thin strip of grass that is cut slightly higher than the putting surface. This strip, which separates the green from surrounding rough, is known as the *fringe*. The fringe is generally mown to the same height as the fairways, and since it's so close to the green, many golfers choose to putt their ball from this condition.

Bunkers

Bunkers are large holes cut in the ground that are filled with sand. Many refer to these hazards as "sand traps," but bunker is the most widely accepted term. Bunkers are strategically placed on the course to capture shots that are misdirected.

Greenside bunkers are located very near the putting surface. These bunkers are usually deeper, with steeper slopes, and a specialized shot is required to escape this sand effectively.

Fairway bunkers can be found flanking the desired landing areas on longer par-4 and par-5 holes. These bunkers are generally shallower and easier to play from than those near the greens.

Water Hazards

Many golf courses feature bodies of water, from small ponds and streams to lakes and even oceans. Water is certainly a valuable golf course resource and very aesthetically pleasing—but very frustrating when your golf ball makes a splash!

Red stakes or paint indicates a lateral water hazard, which will generally run along the side of a golf hole.

Water hazards that you need to hit directly over are marked with yellow stakes or yellow paint.

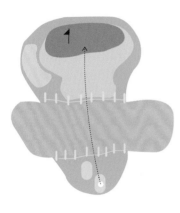

Out of Bounds and Ground Under Repair

Areas on the golf course that have been damaged or are considered abnormal will sometimes be circled with white paint. If your golf ball comes to rest within the painted lines, it's considered to be in ground that is under repair. That paint means that the facility recognizes the situation and allows you to take free relief. You may pick up your ball and drop it within one club-length of the painted line (but not closer to the hole) without a penalty. White stakes indicate "out of bounds," and are usually found at the edges of the golf course property. If your ball goes beyond these stakes, you must replay the shot from where the ball was last struck and add a penalty stroke to your score.

If your ball drops inside the white repair lines on a course, you get free relief. Pick up your ball and drop it within one club-length and continue your game.

types of courses and access limitations

I've described some of the different conditions you will find on a golf course, and I've described how courses differ from one another in terms of design. In this section, I will outline some differences in terms of golf course access. There are college courses and military courses that may limit public play by offering primary access to associated students and members of the military service. But the most common courses you will come across are indicated here.

Public Courses

Also known as "daily fee" courses, these facilities are open to the general public. At these courses you should always call ahead and try to reserve a tee-time, as they can get busy. You will pay to play—usually the higher the green fee, the nicer the course.

Municipal Courses

These facilities are usually operated or managed by officials from the town or city where the course is located. They're usually open to the public but may offer discounted fees to local residents.

Resort Courses

These courses are usually owned and operated by a resort hotel at a popular travel destination. They can be private or semi-private but will allow resort guests to have access. In some cases the green fees are included in a "travel package deal"; otherwise, resort guests would enjoy access and pay green fees when they play.

Semi-Private Courses

These courses offer memberships like a private golf course, but they also allow limited access to the general public. For example, a semi-private course may be open to the public on weekends, but only allow members to play during the week.

Private Courses

Private golf courses allow access only to members of that particular club and their guests. These courses will interview potential members. If accepted, a new member will typically pay an initiation fee and annual dues. As a member, they would not have to pay green fees. The general public is not allowed to play a private course unless they are the guest of a member in good standing.

The courses are all regulation-length, or championship courses. Other options include "pitch and putts," courses that only have par-3 holes, and small "executive courses" that have short par 4s and par 3s. There are driving ranges, miniature golf courses, and even golf simulators that you can try on a rainy day. Golf comes in many forms—there is always a way to enjoy this great game!

The club house of GlenArbor Golf Club. This beautiful private course in Bedford Hills, New York, is where all of the photos in this book were taken.

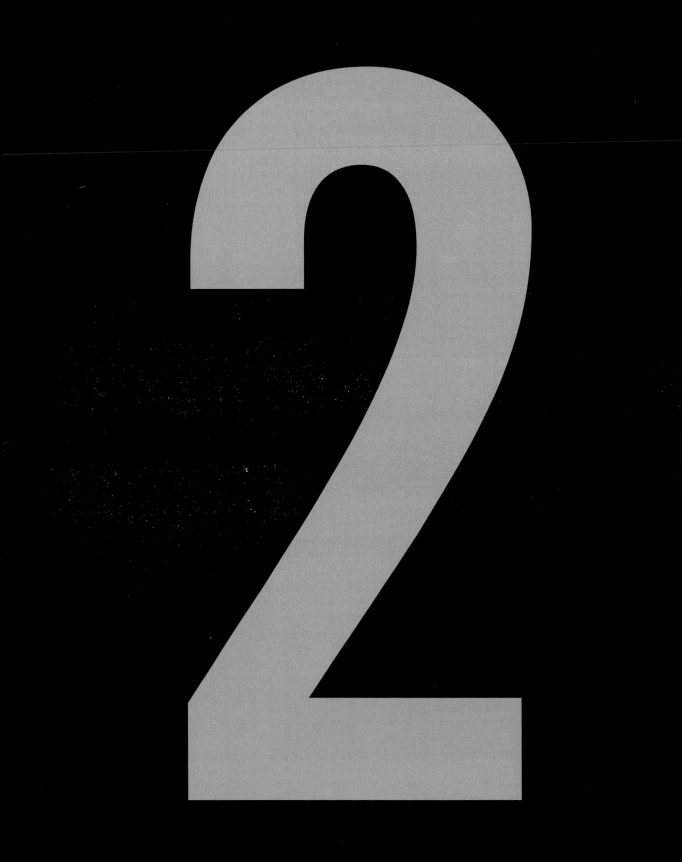

getting into the swing

the setup

Although you aren't dribbling up and down a court, running the bases, or breaking tackles downfield, your golf swing is a very athletic motion that requires a stable base. That stable base is known as your stance, or address position. But there's more to a good swing than just a stable stance. In construction terms, the golf swing is a house, and the grip and address position represent the foundation. In this chapter, we're going to look at all the elements that make up a great setup.

the grip

Before I cover the key points of the address position, we need to discuss the only contact point between you and the golf club—your grip.

Gripping the golf club properly is a very important part of the setup. A good grip will maintain consistent control, yet allow the club to move properly throughout the swing. There are several common grip styles we will review, but in all cases, both hands should feel comfortable on the club and work together as a team. If one hand becomes too dominant, the movement of the club will be erratic. I strongly encourage beginning golfers to practice your chosen grip often. Even practicing your grip position on a club at home while watching TV is very beneficial. Let's take a look at the two-part process of applying your grip.

Here's a look at the grip without a glove. The grip starts with the fingers. Place the club so that it rests on your fingers, not in your palm. Then, close your hand over it.

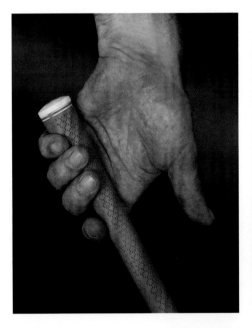

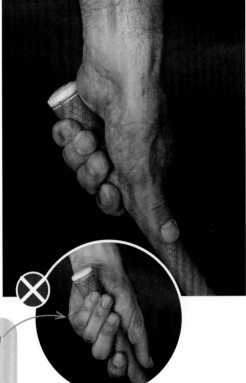

This is the wrong way—the club is sitting too far "up" in the palm.

Step 1:

Place the grip of the club in your left hand as shown. Notice that the grip takes place more toward the fingers than the center of the palm. Approximately ½" of the grip should extend through your hand and beyond your pinkie finger. Then gently close your hand and place your left thumb on the club. Don't wrap the thumb around the side of the grip, but rather align it with the club shaft; this will allow for support at the top of your backswing.

Step 2:

Now place your right hand on the club below your left hand. The palm of your right hand should fit neatly over your left thumb. As with the left hand, you should feel the club more in your fingers than in your palm. The precise position of the pinkie finger on your right hand depends upon which grip style you choose (see the next spread), but the other fingers should be in contact with the club. Your right thumb should then be applied to the club in a position that hides the left thumb and rests on the shaft as shown.

In a standard or "neutral" grip position, the creases (sometimes referred to as the "v"s) that are formed between the thumb and forefinger of each hand should point toward your right shoulder. A "strong" grip position doesn't refer to your hand strength, it refers to a position where those creases point behind the right shoulder. The strong grip has a tendency to "close" the clubface easier during the swing, resulting in shots that head to the left of your target line. In a "weak" grip position, the creases will point closer to the left shoulder. With a weak grip position, the clubface tends to remain "open" through impact, resulting in shots that start to the right of your target line. I recommend the neutral or standard position.

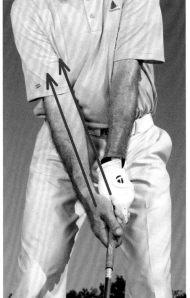

The Most Common Grips

There are three full-swing grip styles in golf. These styles differ from each other due to the positioning of the right pinkie finger. One isn't more "correct" than the other—it really is all about what works best for you.

The Overlap Grip

To create this grip, the right pinkie finger rests in the valley formed between the left index and middle fingers. This helps to cement the two hands together, and encourages them to work as one. The overlap may feel a bit odd at first, but it's likely the most common grip and I would recommend this style for most players.

The Interlock Grip

Players with smaller fingers may benefit from using the interlock grip. With this grip, the right pinkie actually weaves between the left index finger and the left middle finger. Although this grip removes both the left index finger and the right pinkie finger from the club, some players prefer this style.

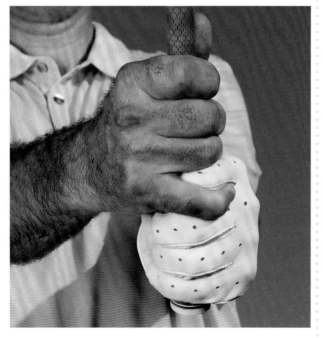
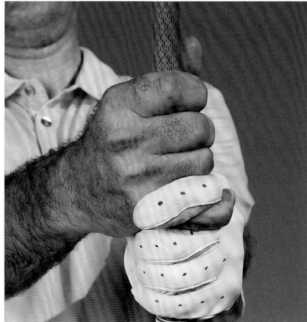

The Baseball or Ten-Finger Grip

This grip style is fairly popular with beginners and golfers with smaller hands. It's named the baseball grip because all eight fingers are in contact with the club, similar to a grip you would take on a baseball bat. This style is also referred to as the 10-finger grip because every finger contacts the club (and obviously, this counts the thumbs as fingers). Although I encourage you to try the "overlap" grip first, some feel a greater sense of control and confidence with this grip style.

Regardless of the grip style you choose, be sure that your hands are working together as a single unit—you should not feel one hand overpowering the other. Additionally, it's important to keep consistent grip pressure during your swing. If you hold the club too loosely, it could shift in your hands during the swing or at impact. But hold it too tightly, and your muscles will tense and prohibit you from making a smooth and very repeatable motion. On a scale of 0 to 10 (10 being "white-knuckle" squeezing), I would recommend somewhere around a 6.

A good analogy for grip pressure is to imagine holding the club as if you were squeezing a tube of toothpaste—firm enough to push the paste out, but not so firm as to make a mess.

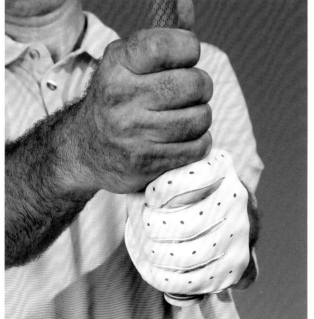

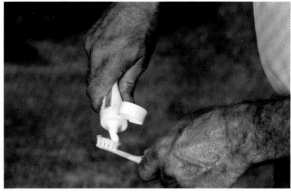

taking a stance

It's important to have proper posture and body position prior to each swing. The better your stance (or *address position*), the better your chances for a successful golf swing. The stance is really your starting point for each swing, and it's comprised of several basic elements.

Shoulders

Although as a right-handed player your right shoulder will be a bit lower than your left (see the previous section on grip), a line drawn across your chest from shoulder to shoulder should be parallel to a line drawn across your hips, knees, and toes.

Weight Distribution

This varies based on which type of shot you're taking, but for general purposes, your weight should be evenly distributed between each foot, and the bulk of the pressure should be under the laces of your shoes. You should avoid too much weight on the heels or toes.

Feet

For the typical full swing, you want your feet shoulder-width apart, and they should be splayed or angled out just a touch. Many beginners point their feet straight forward as if they were skiing, but rotating each foot out a bit (distance between toes should be slightly greater than distance between heels) will help to support a more powerful golf swing.

Head/Chin

Don't "bury" your chin into your chest (a common result of trying too hard to "keep your head down"); there should be some space. Imagine there's an orange under your chin—that space is helpful. You'll need that room later to make a comfortable shoulder turn.

Arms

Resist the temptation to "reach" out toward the ball. Your arms should hang naturally from your shoulders. If the rest of your address position is proper, you should see that your hands are hanging freely and should be a couple inches clear (and in front) of your thighs.

Hips

Bend forward from the hips, keeping your spine relatively straight. If done properly, your belt buckle should point down toward the ground. Those who "slouch" down to the ball improperly have a belt line that's fairly horizontal and parallel with the horizon.

Knees

Your knees should be flexed a bit. Straight legs will not allow for a powerful or consistent swing. But don't bend your knees too much—just a little flex as shown.

ball position

After taking your address position, you'll find that the distance between you and the ball varies depending on which club you're holding. Clubs vary in length. Your wedges are significantly shorter than your fairway woods and driver. Your arms should always hang down comfortably from your shoulders, so the longer the club, the farther you will be from the ball. Get in the habit of taking your same stance, then letting the length of the club dictate how far you need to be from the ball.

No, I'm not playing three balls at once! This is just to illustrate how the length of the club shaft dictates your distance from the ball.

After determining how far you need to be from the ball, you need to position the ball properly in your stance. A general guide would be:

Wedges: Center of the stance

Irons: Closer to the target, 1 inch (2.5cm) forward of center

Hybrids/fairway woods: 2 inches (5cm) forward of center

Driver: Just inside your left heel

For a strong visual, imagine how a ridiculously long club would force you to set up your stance!

taking aim

Now that you've established a good grip, an effective stance, and proper ball position, it's time to take aim! Taking aim in basketball is easy, taking aim in billiards is easy, and taking aim with a rifle is, yes, relatively easy. In all of these cases, your line of sight is directly in line with your target. In golf, an imaginary line drawn from the ball to the intended landing spot is called a *target line*. Although the intent is for the ball to travel to the target similar to other sports, in golf you must stand to the side of that line. Since you're unable to look directly down the target line, it's considerably more difficult to assess whether or not you're aligned properly for the upcoming shot.

The important thing to remember is that a properly aligned setup will position your feet parallel to the target line. In other words, a line drawn from the toe of your right shoe to the toe of your left shoe will be parallel to the direction you expect the ball to travel. In fact, imaginary lines across your knees, hips, shoulders, and forearms should *all* be parallel to the target line as shown below.

Golf is played and enjoyed by people of all shapes and sizes, but it's important to note that those who are physically fit and fairly flexible do have an edge. If you have any injuries or specific physical weaknesses (back, knees, elbows, wrists, etc.), you should check with your doctor before taking serious swings.

Practicing Your Alignment

To practice this proper alignment (whish is also known as setting up "square"), it's very helpful to set up an alignment station. Set an alignment rod (or a golf club) parallel to the target line and just outside the ball. Then set another parallel rod or club closer to your feet. Set up a station like this when you practice. The more you get accustomed to setting up square and making swings in this parallel station, the more likely you'll be to align yourself properly with your targets on the golf course.

Squaring your clubface with the target line is essential—and it's much easier to do when you use the parallel alignment station. Now that you've set up properly, it's time to take a swing!

A "closed" clubface will launch the ball left of the target line.

An "open" clubface will launch the ball to the right of the target line.

A club has been positioned squarely behind the ball when the leading edge of that clubface is perpendicular to the target line. A ball struck with a square clubface will be propelled toward the target.

the full swing

A round of golf features many different types of swings, from little putts to big, full shots. In this section you're going to learn the swing most people identify with golf—the full swing. The full swing is the foundation of your golf game— you'll use it from the tee and all along the fairway.

Since each club has its own type of full swing, I've broken down this section by club, starting with the swings from the tee with your longest clubs to your swings as you get closer to the cup. You will notice some common threads among these swings—all of them feature a solid address position, and highlight the importance of staying centered and being balanced at the finish. However, even though the swings are similar, there are some very important differences from one club to the next. In addition to the key positions of the swings and the entire swing sequence, you'll also find helpful visual aids, some other aspects you need to consider when executing a swing, and practice drills to help perfect your swing. So get out your driver, and let's get started!

the driver swing

If you haven't heard the adage "Drive for show—putt for dough," I can guarantee that you'll hear it soon. It's a very common phrase on the golf course. Those words are usually mumbled by an envious golfer just after seeing another player in his group bomb a massive tee shot down the fairway. The true meaning of that bittersweet statement is "Sure, you just hit a great drive, but the golfer who putts the best usually wins the match." Yes, putting is important, but the drive sets the tone for the rest of the hole. Trust me, hitting the "long ball" well is not only a key to better scoring, it's also one of the most satisfying shots in golf!

The driver is typically the longest club in the bag, and is designed to hit the ball farther down the fairway than any other club. Since it's expected to hit the ball the farthest, the driver is the most popular and commonly used club at driving ranges everywhere. On the golf course, players frequently use the driver on longer holes that require significant distance from the opening shot (par 4s and par 5s). Unfortunately, most players want that extra distance too much. They swing too hard, which causes a loss of form and balance and leads to mis-hits and poor results.

With a good setup and a relaxed, balanced swing, the driver will help you cover a lot of ground without using too much effort—and quickly become one of your favorite clubs in the bag.

The Setup

The foundation of a great swing is your setup, or address. Here are the key points of a perfect address.

The ball should be on a tee and positioned just inside the left heel.

You need a stable base, with feet shoulder width apart.

Hands (grip) should be in line with the ball and positioned "left of the zipper."

The spine should tilt slightly away from the target.

Relax the shoulders, and the left shoulder should be higher than the right.

Your head should be positioned behind the ball.

Weight distribution should favor the right side a bit (55 percent right, 45 percent left).

Since it's the longest club, the driver stance requires you to be farther from the ball at address.

Although the ball is forward in your stance, be sure that the shoulders are parallel to the target line.

Forearms, hips, knee line, and toe line should also be parallel to the intended target line.

Knees should be flexed slightly and arms should hang comfortably, allowing space between hands and thighs.

Although you're farther from the ball with a driver swing, be careful not to bend down and "reach" too much for the ball. Maintain balance with a comfortable tilt of the spine.

Key Positions of the Swing

Begin the Backswing

Sweep the club up (don't lift it) to this position, keeping the clubhead moving a bit faster than the hands. Let the "hinge" (the angle) between the club shaft and the left forearm increase. As you bring the driver around the tilted axis (your spine), allow the clubface to open naturally. Although the hips are beginning to rotate, the shoulders are turning at a faster rate, which begins to create coil for power later in the swing.

Top of the Backswing

At the top of the backswing your shoulders should be fully turned, with the left shoulder behind the ball and your back facing the target. At this point the club shaft should be nearly parallel to the ground (although if you're not that flexible it may be less than parallel, which is fine). Your left arm should still be long; resist the temptation to hinge your left elbow. Your weight should now feel farther to the right, but should remain on the instep of your right foot.

Downswing and Impact

As you bring the club back down in the same sweeping motion, transfer your weight back to the left side as your hips rotate through the impact zone. Your belt buckle should be pointing in front of the ball before making contact. Although your hips are rotating past the ball, take note that your shoulders are square with the target line and your chest is facing the ball. Your hands have returned squarely to the ball with a long left arm, and your head is still clearly behind the ball.

Finish

At the finish, you should feel that nearly all of your weight is now on your left side—it should be toward the outside of your left heel. Although there will still be some spine tilt at the finish (see inset), your hips have rotated so that your belt buckle is pointing to (or even left of) your target, and your right pocket is now over your left foot. You should be able to pose and hold this finish position.

Swing Sequence (Front)

Here is how the entire swing should look from the front:

Don't bury your chin into your chest.

Your left shoulder should be lower than your right at this point.

Maintain spine tilt–don't get taller during backswing.

Maintain some flex in your right knee.

Try to keep the left heel grounded, but if you're less flexible you can lift it a bit.

Keep your right elbow pointed toward the ground.

Swing Sequence (Side)

Here is how the entire swing should look from the side:

Watch the angle between the left forearm and the club shaft.

Your right elbow should be very close to the right hip, and lower than the left elbow.

Your right shoulder should now be lower than the left.

You should feel like you're hitting the ball on the upswing, not making a descending blow.

Your eyes are still focused on the ball at impact.

Your spine is still tilted slightly away from the target, and your head starts to swivel so you can pick up the flight of the ball.

Maintain your spine angle through impact.

Your arms are long and relaxed.

Notice the forearms have rotated naturally.

Seeing the entire sole of the right foot at this point is proof of a nice finish.

"Pose for the camera." Great balance here is an indicator that your swing is firing in the proper sequence.

Additional Considerations

Tee Height

When teed up at the ideal height, the crown or top edge of the driver would bisect the equator of the golf ball. Teeing the ball at this height encourages a "no divot" strike, which actually feels like you're sweeping the ball off the tee on the upswing. If you're driving into a stiff wind, you may want to tee it lower to encourage a lower, more penetrating ball flight.

Distance from the Ball

Since the driver is the longest club, it's difficult to see if the ball is centered in the middle of the clubface at address. In fact, what appears to be centered may actually be closer to the heel. Stand behind your ball and place the club in the perfect position, then carefully go back to address. Centered may appear to be closer to the toe of the club than you thought. Good to know!

This tee is set too high   This tee is set too low

Where to Tee It Up

If your ball tends to fade, slice, or "bend to the right," there's an advantage to teeing up on the right side of the teeing ground and aiming for the left side of the fairway. Conversely, if you draw or hook the ball, you should tee the ball closer to the left tee marker and aim for the right side of the fairway. This adjustment effectively widens your landing area significantly. Try it!

Choking Down for Accuracy

If you're faced with a very narrow fairway surrounded by deep rough, and you really want to keep it in the short grass, you can tee the ball a bit lower and choke down on your driver a couple inches. To accommodate the change, you'll need to get a little closer to the ball at address. This will increase your accuracy (but cost you a little yardage). You can also consider teeing off with a fairway wood or a hybrid on holes that demand greater accuracy.

Common Mistakes

You now understand the basics of teeing off with the driver. But following are some common mistakes to watch out for when you're swinging "the big stick."

The "Flying" Right Elbow

With the excitement of hitting the long ball, many beginners yank the club up quickly, and the right elbow becomes too separated from the body. This flying right elbow can lead to serious inconsistency.

Remember to turn your shoulders as you take the club back, and try to keep the elbow more connected and closer to your body.

Swinging Off the Back Foot

Even players who take the club back beautifully can get anxious and start their downswing too violently, moving their arms and shoulders too fast and leaving too much weight on the back foot.

Remember to transfer your weight steadily from the inside of the back (right) foot to your left side through impact. Your belt buckle should be rotating past the ball before the club gets to the ball.

Picture This!

Swinging Under the Foam

This is my own variation of an idea made popular by Ben Hogan. I've cut a hole in a 2'x8' (.5 × 2.5m) sheet of foam insulation and allowed it to drop onto my shoulders at address. The best golf swings move on a tilted plane. This image illustrates how a driver moving properly will swing back under the foam, then down through the ball under the foam. Keep this image in mind for a better driver swing!

Eye on the Chest

Many golfers rush their downswing with the driver and rotate their shoulders too quickly and too early. Imagine there's an eyeball in your chest. Although you're rotating your hips and beginning to shift weight, your chest should be "looking" at the ball at impact. This image will help you to be more patient with your shoulders and make better contact with the driver.

Practice Drill 1: The Headcover Drill

So many golfers want to swing too hard with the driver, which leads to fast, tense arms that move too rapidly. This is a great drill that helps to synchronize the arms with the turn of the body. Place your friend's headcover under your right arm as you take your address position. Then make just a half swing back and a half swing through, keeping the headcover in position under your arm. You'll feel your body and arms working together, and the club will move very consistently around you. This little drill should be done with just small half swings, and should help you feel a more connected swing. If the headcover drops, you're not moving in the proper sequence. After taking a few practice swings like this, try the drill with a ball, and ultimately try some full swings without the headcover. Just keep that connected feeling as you turn through the ball.

Practice Drill 2: The Water Bottle

Here's a very simple drill that will help to create a consistent and powerful swing path. Set up a station at the range that has two alignment aids (other clubs will be fine), one to help with a parallel foot line and one as a guide just outside, but parallel to, your target line. Then position a plastic water bottle about 1 foot (30.5cm) behind the ball and just inside the outer alignment guide as shown. A golfer who gets too anxious or swings too violently with his arms is likely to go outside the proper swing path, and will hit the bottle. With a centered and relaxed swing, the club will move from the top of the backswing through impact without endangering the bottle. Put a tee where the ball should be and try to sweep through the tee without touching the bottle. After a few successful practice swings, put a ball on the tee and enjoy the results!

fairway woods and hybrids

Although these clubs are no longer made of wood, the name has stuck. You may hear them referred to as "fairway metals" once in a while, but "fairway woods" is the most accepted term. They won't hit the ball quite as far as the driver, but fairway woods are designed to give you plenty of distance. They're often a good option from the teeing ground on short par-4 holes, very long par 3s, and on any hole where accuracy seems more important than power. As their name implies, fairway woods are also very useful from the fairway, and provide more distance than irons. Since the face of a fairway wood has more loft than a driver, players can sweep the ball clean off the "deck" (turf) without the use of a tee.

Hybrids are included in this section because in many ways they're similar to fairway woods. Although slightly shorter in overall length, the hybrid has a clubhead that looks like a smaller (and more lofted) version of a fairway wood. Hybrids are sometimes referred to as "long iron replacements" because many players have removed the 3-, 4-, and 5-irons from their set in favor of hybrid clubs. Hybrids are much more forgiving than long irons, and also allow players to get the ball up in the air easier and escape light rough without sacrificing distance.

From the fairway or from the tee, fairway woods and hybrid clubs offer the golfer a very useful combination of distance and accuracy.

The Setup

The ball should be positioned approximately 2 inches (5cm) inside the left heel (if playing from a tee, the ball could be slightly closer to the target).

Your feet should be shoulder width apart.

Hands should be positioned in line with the ball.

Your spine tilts slightly away from the target, left shoulder higher than right.

The left arm should be "long" and both arms relaxed.

Your weight should feel like it's favoring your right side a bit.

These clubs are shorter than the driver, so you'll be slightly closer to the ball at address.

The shoulders, forearms, knees, and toe line are all parallel to target line.

Bend forward from the waist, keeping the spine relatively straight—don't curve or "hunch" down to the ball.

Your arms should hang relaxed and extend out a bit naturally—don't "reach" for the ball.

Your weight should not press too much to the heels or toes; it should feel like your weight is "under the laces" of your shoes.

Key Positions of the Swing

Begin the Backswing

Up to this point your shoulders should do most of the work. Use them to turn the club and the arms back to this position. Your backswing should be more of a rotational motion around the spine, not a lateral hip motion that would cause the right leg to straighten. You should keep your right leg leaning toward the target a bit and not appear vertical. Your left arm should remain as long as it was at address.

Top of the Backswing

When you complete your backswing, your left shoulder should be turned fully and positioned behind the ball. Your right leg should not straighten, and stays angled toward the target. Your left arm is still long, which leads to greater consistency and more power. This full turn has taken place without sacrificing spine tilt. You should maintain the height you had at address. Resist the temptation to rise or straighten up during the backswing.

Downswing and Impact

At this critical impact position, you should be shifting weight to the right side as your hips rotate toward the target. The swing with these longer clubs requires smooth acceleration. Your left arm should be long at impact for best results. If you "yank" the club down to the ball too quickly, you'll create a bent left arm at this point. Your hands have traveled just past the position they had at address (the club should be vertical or leaning just a touch toward the target). For fairway woods and hybrids it is paramount to keep your head behind the ball at impact, which leads to a clean, sweeping impact.

Finish

These clubs will help you hit the ball great distances, but resist the temptation to swing too hard. Your weight should now be entirely on your left side, and just the toe of your right shoe should be touching the ground. You should be able to hold this stable finish position comfortably; if you swing like a gorilla, you'll probably lose your balance.

Swing Sequence (Front)

Here is how the entire swing should look from the front:

With these longer clubs it's important to remember that they travel around your body, not up vertically.

The toe of the club should be pointing almost straight up.

Although your head may swivel a bit during the backswing, your eyes should still be focused on the ball.

The left arm stays extended, as long it was at address.

The angle between the club shaft and the left forearm shows that you have fully "hinged" or cocked your wrists.

Swing Sequence (Side)

Here is how the entire swing should look from the side:

Unwind your hips and rotate them toward the target faster than your shoulders.

The club should be returning on the same path it took during the backswing.

The grip end of the club should be pointing in the direction of the ball.

You can see both back pockets, which means the hips have turned aggressively through the downswing; the hips have turned through quicker than the shoulders.

Keep your head behind the ball at impact.

The right foot should be coming off the ground as weight continues to transfer to the left side.

Your belt buckle should be nearly facing the target.

No tension in the arms—the force of the swing should extend them fully at this point.

Your spine should still be tilted slightly away from target.

Those with good flexibility will have their chest actually facing left of the target at this point (don't worry if you're not all the way there).

Great balance will lead to consistent results.

A relaxed swing will allow the club to complete its journey through the ball and to finish behind you as shown.

Additional Considerations

Rough Lies

Although they're an option with a great lie in the rough, fairway woods are best used from ... you guessed it, the fairway. If you need distance, and your ball is in the rough, it's best to switch to a hybrid club. For deeper rough, sacrifice some distance and use a more lofted hybrid. For the ugliest and deepest rough, forget these longer clubs. Chop your ball out with a wedge!

The Good Lie

A good "lie" in the fairway equals a greater opportunity for distance.

Fairway woods come in different lengths and lofts, and the longer the club, the lower the loft (and the farther your ball will travel). The most common: 3-wood (approximately 15 degrees of loft), 5-wood (approximately 19 degrees), and 7-wood (approximately 24 degrees). A 3-wood will hit the ball the farthest, but you need a good and fairly level lie in the fairway. If the ground is uneven, it would be best to select a club with more loft. When you're in the rough, hybrids are usually the better choice.

That's How the Ball Rolls

These longer clubs generally hit the ball lower. The ball flies a long way in the air, but it will also roll a long way on the ground after it lands (especially in dry conditions). Keep in mind that a ball traveling a long distance will be difficult to stop. If you hit the green, the ball may roll across the surface into rough or other trouble on the far side. When hitting out of light rough, the ball has even less spin and is likely to roll even farther. Choose your club carefully—you may need to land in front of the green and let the ball roll onto the putting surface.

Common Mistakes

There are two common mistakes that can lead to poor contact—especially with these longer clubs. Be wary of the "trouble" positions below. If you mimic my proper form, you'll be on your way to better contact.

Standing Up During the Backswing

One of the most common flaws in golf is rising up during the backswing. Straightening up and changing the spine angle you had at address (making it more vertical) will lead to very inconsistent results. Players who increase their height like this are likely to top the ball.

If you maintain your height from address to the top of your backswing, your spine angle will stay consistent. Turning around a stable axis, the spine, will help you hit the ball cleanly more often. Notice how the shoulders rotate around that axis. At the top, the right shoulder should be higher than the left.

Steering the Ball

Many players try to steer the ball rather than swing through it. They're very concerned with hitting the ball straight and they hold on to the club too firmly. But trying to keep the clubface pointed at the target too long will rob you of valuable distance.

Don't try to guide the ball to your target. During a relaxed and powerful swing, the clubface will gradually rotate open (clubface points to the right of the target) on the way back, and rotate closed (to the left of the target) on the way through as shown. Allowing the club to move naturally like this will produce plenty of distance, and more accuracy than you might expect.

Picture This!

The Ceiling

After taking your comfortable address position, imagine there's a ceiling that appears just above your head. This image will help you maintain your spine angle and turn rather than lift. Avoid bumping your head on the ceiling, and you'll start hitting better shots.

Ping-Pong Paddle

It's easy to get caught up in hitting the ball straight, but releasing the club properly is one of the secrets to both consistency and power. This Ping-Pong paddle has a red side and a black side. Imagine you're swinging the paddle—first you see black, then you see red; it opens and closes. The face of your golf club should do the same. This image will help you release the club properly.

Practice Drill 1: The Alignment Rod

Take your normal stance at address, then firmly hold an alignment rod or even a golf club across your shoulders as shown. Maintain your spine angle as you make your shoulder turn. A full turn should point the rod at a spot behind the ball. If you maintain proper spine angle, you'll notice that the rod not only points behind the ball, but also stays on an angle (since your left shoulder should be lower than your right at the completion of the backswing). Practice this drill in both directions. You'll get a good feel for how your body should turn, and also improve your flexibility.

Practice Drill 2: The Cold Shoulder

This drill will help you keep your shoulders from over-rotating through impact. While taking a comfortable stance, extend your left arm and position it atop a long club just outside your intended target line. Next, grab a shorter club with your right hand and place it in a typical address position. Now take some half swings with just one hand, being careful to stay "inside" the vertical club. This drill accomplishes a couple of things. First, it forces you to be more patient with your shoulders. It also encourages a nice feel for releasing the club with your right hand. After a few practice swings, tee up a ball and swing right through it.

irons and wedges

Irons are the most common clubs found in a golf bag. Everyone remembers a booming drive or that critical putt, but most swings on a golf course are made with irons. Irons don't hit the ball as far as a driver, or fairway woods or hybrids, but they tend to have the greatest control and accuracy. They're numbered, and the higher the iron number, the higher and shorter they'll cause the ball to fly.

As recently as 25 years ago, you could find 1-irons and 2-irons in play on the course, but in recent years most low-numbered or "long irons" have been replaced by hybrid clubs. Today, a typical set will include a 5-, 6-, 7-, 8-, and 9-iron along with a pitching wedge (PW) and a sand wedge (SW)—the shortest and most lofted irons. Irons are commonly used on shorter par-3 holes and for approach shots—shots when you're trying to make the ball land (and stay) on the green. Because irons have more loft and grooves in their faces, they launch the ball higher and apply more backspin, which helps to keep the ball from rolling off the putting surface. If you miss the green, your wedges and most lofted irons are used to chip or pitch your ball onto the green from close range. The following pages reveal the secrets to a successful iron swing.

The Setup

front

side

Left hand higher on the club equals left shoulder higher than right shoulder.

Your head should be just slightly behind the ball.

Feet should be shoulder-width apart.

Your weight is evenly distributed on each foot.

The ball is positioned in center for wedges/short irons, 1 inch (2.5cm) ahead of center for mid-irons (8-, 7-, and 6-iron), and 2 inches (5cm) ahead of center for long irons (5-, 4-, and 3-iron).

Hands should be slightly ahead of the ball.

With these shorter clubs, you'll be closer to the ball at address.

Arms should hang comfortably from the shoulders, leaving some space between grip and thighs.

Note the angle between forearms and club shaft: this should *not* be a straight line.

Square address position with feet, knees, hips, forearms, and shoulders all parallel to the target line.

Key Positions of the Swing

Begin the Backswing

The backswing begins with the clubhead, arms, and shoulders moving away from the ball. At this point, the clubhead and shaft should be on an angle above your left forearm. Your grip pressure should be consistent and firm enough to move the club to this position comfortably. If your grip is too loose, the clubhead will lag below your arms and your tempo and timing will suffer.

Top of the Backswing

Your hips have rotated and your belt buckle should be facing behind the ball at this point, but your shoulders should be turned to a much greater degree. Remain centered as you make this rotational turn to the top. Take care not to sway away from the ball with your hips. If done correctly you'll see that the right leg is braced and still angled toward the target as it was at address.

Impact

Many call this the moment of truth. To achieve the best results with irons, your hands must pass the ball before the club makes contact. The shaft should now be leaning forward, which indicates a descending blow. The club should strike the ball on its way down and through, leading to a divot after impact. This downward strike is critical for successful iron shots.

Finish

As with all golf swings, an iron or wedge shot should finish in total balance. Nearly all of your weight should now be on your left side. The sole of your right shoe should be totally visible. Proper rotation of the hips will lead to a finish with your knees close together as shown. Do not attempt to keep your head down— at this point you should be able to follow the flight of your ball.

Swing Sequence (Front)

Here is how the entire swing should look from the front:

The clubhead should be traveling to the inside of the ball as you turn, not straight back on the target line.

The back of the left wrist forms a straight line with the left forearm.

Swing Sequence (Side)

Here is how the entire swing should look from the side:

The club shaft should appear between the forearms.

If it's in line with the left arm, it's too steep; if it's below the right forearm, it's too shallow.

Hands should be slightly ahead of the ball.

Remember to strike the "little ball" (golf ball) before the "big ball" (Earth).

Your chest is pointing toward the ball, and your hips should have rotated more to the left at impact.

Your right heel should be off the ground, and your weight is rotated to the left side.

You should have no tension in your arms—they're swinging freely through to the finish.

Your body has rotated through the shot, and a nearly vertical left leg is supporting your weight.

Additional Considerations

Divots

The most critical thing to remember with an iron or wedge swing is that down equals up. It seems contradictory, but in order to hit beautiful, high iron shots, your club needs to descend through impact. The loft of the iron will launch it skyward as you swing down through the ball. If you try to lift the ball into the sky, you'll often hit the ground behind the ball first, resulting in a "fat" shot that causes a deep divot and very poor distance. Attempting to lift can also cause a "thin" shot, which occurs when the club rises into the middle of the ball, strikes near the equator, and rockets the ball on a line-drive over the green. In the bottom-left photo, a tee in the ground is marking the position of the ball prior to contact. Having delivered a downward strike, you'll notice that the ball has taken flight and my club has taken a divot on the target side of the tee. The ball is contacted first, *before* striking the ground. The bottom of the iron/wedge swing is truly in front of the ball.

Divot Diagnosis

A divot is the mark your club leaves in the ground after a swing. Where the divot points can tell you a lot about your swing. To get very accurate feedback, you should first indicate a line (with another club or an alignment rod) that is parallel to and outside of your target line. Then address the ball with your feet parallel to the alignment aid and make your swing. The divot you leave will be pointing in one of three directions:

Parallel, or straight toward the target: In this case, the swing plane is in very good shape. The club has been delivered to the ball on a very nice path. And since the club is traveling from behind the player to the ball, that path will move from "inside to out" naturally. Of course the clubface could be aiming a little right, or a little left, but generally even your misses will be pretty good shots!

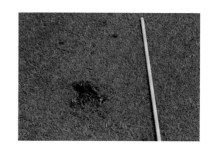

To the left of the target: This divot is very common. In this case, the player's energy is moving too far to the left. A divot facing this direction is the result of a swing that is "over the top," meaning the clubface travels from outside the target line, through the ball and too far to the left of the target. The ball will either fly straight but to the left (a "pull"), left to further left (a "pull-hook"), or left to right (a "slice"), depending on where the clubface is pointing at impact. With energy traveling too far to the left like this, the "slice" is the only shot that could get the ball to the target.

To the right of the target: This divot is made by a player who swings too far from the inside, or "inside to out." This energy path is moving dramatically from well inside the target line to way out to the right. A swing that makes this divot will launch a ball straight but to the right (a "push"), right to further right (a "push-slice"), or right to left (a "hook"), depending on where the club is facing at impact. With this much energy moving right and outside, the "hook" is the only trajectory that could fly the ball back to the target.

Common Mistakes

I've highlighted two common full-swing flaws that will keep you from playing your best. Mimic the proper positions and you'll hit more greens!

The Chicken Wing

This common flaw shows up when a golfer is too anxious to hit the ball and begins the downswing with the left arm. This "chicken wing" position also occurs with players who fear hitting the ground first or have trouble taking a proper divot.

The left arm should be "long" at impact. Provided you are turning the hips through impact and getting your weight to the left side, the long left arm will help you hit the ball much more consistently (and you won't have to worry about "topping" the ball or hitting "thin" shots).

Sliding Knees

Some golfers "slide" their knees and/or hips away from the ball during the backswing. Although this may feel like you're getting your weight behind the ball and preparing for a big hit, this is actually a very ineffective position.

A proper backswing features a stable base. Although the right knee does have some flex, it's not sliding away from the ball. The right leg stays strong and actually leans toward the target to help deliver maximum power to the ball.

Picture This!

Taped Arms

This image has been very helpful for golfers who separate their elbows excessively during the backswing ("flying right elbow") or at impact (the "chicken wing"). Imagining that your forearms are bound at address as shown can help to keep your swing more connected. The space between your elbows should remain fairly consistent, especially through the bottom of your swing (halfway down to halfway through).

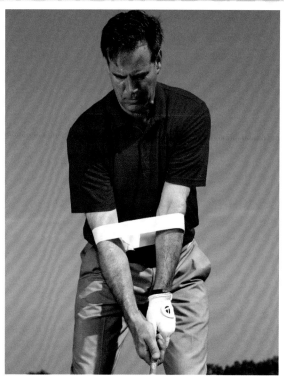

Eye on the Knee

For golfers who rotate their hips too much or slide their knees during the backswing, this image can be of serious value. Imagine there's an eye that looks out from your right knee. During a strong backswing, that eye will continue to look straight forward, as it did at address. If you can keep your right knee from "looking" farther away from the target, you'll hit the ball cleaner and longer!

Practice Drill 1: The Forearm Ball

In the swing sequence earlier in this chapter, you can see the look of a proper release. Just after impact, the arms look relaxed and extended, and a natural rotation has taken place. Players who "hold" or "steer" the club, or try to keep the clubface pointing at the target too long after impact, will never feel comfortable. After putting a ball between your forearms, make some practice swings—just halfway back (left arm feels long) to halfway through (right arm feels long). You should feel a natural rotation taking place, and your body will turn more effectively.

Try hitting some balls off a tee with this drill—small swings only. If you do this drill properly, you'll feel more connected and you won't drop the ball.

Practice Drill 2: The Shadow

Most golfers struggle with consistency. One of the leading causes of inconsistency is swaying, a lateral motion that moves the center of your swing back and forth. The shadow drill trains a golfer to stay centered from address to the top of the backswing, and back to impact.

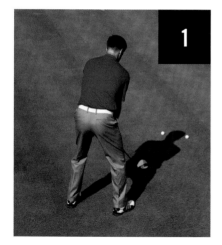  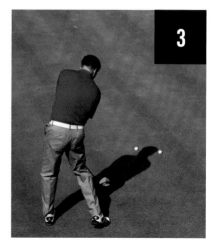

Step 1: Take your address with the sun at your back after placing two balls on the ground in front of you. The balls should be about 1 foot (30cm) apart, and the head of your shadow should be positioned between them.

Step 2: As you take your backswing, watch and make sure your shadow stays between the balls.

Step 3: As you return the club to impact, your shadow should still be in place. If you were to take a full swing, your shadow should move beyond the front ball after impact, but for now, focus on the centered feeling you'll get from making a full turn and returning to impact without swaying out of position!

shots around the green

When asked to imagine a golfer in action, most people picture the big, sweeping motion of a full swing. And most golfers spend the bulk of their practice time pounding drives and swinging out of their shoes. Ironically, the overwhelming majority of shots played in a typical round, occur within 100 yards of the flag. As you first start to play this game, you'll quickly find that perfect full swings don't occur as often as you'd like. The key to improvement and future success is learning how to recover from your misses. And the best way to save strokes is with successful recovery shots from just off the putting surface. If you begin your golf career understanding the importance of these shorter shots, you'll definitely have an edge.

The following pages will show you the necessary technique required to chip the ball effectively, hit delicate pitch shots, and blast out of sand bunkers with ease. Many of the world's best golfers practice chipping and pitching in their own backyards—and you should spend time working on these shots as well! Pay close attention to the instruction and drills in this chapter. Developing "feel" and "touch" around the green will quickly lead you to lower scores!

chipping

In golf, an "approach" is a shot that is expected to land on the putting surface. Regardless of skill level or experience, the closer you are to the flag, the better your chances of finding your target—and the higher your expectations. But it's common for even the very best players to miss the green.

A chip shot is frequently used when you're close (usually 10 yards [9m] away or less) but haven't yet found the putting surface. The chip is a low-trajectory shot that travels farther on the ground after it lands than it does in the air. A great chip features a much smaller motion than a full swing, but will propel the ball far enough to land on or very close to the green. After landing, the ball should hop forward and continue to roll toward the flag. You can chip from a variety of conditions; the fairway, the fringe of the green, even from the rough if you have a nice lie. You can also chip with a number of different clubs (for more information on clubs, see the following "additional considerations" section). In this chapter, you'll learn the basics of this very important shot.

The Setup

front

side

The ball is positioned toward the back foot (behind center).

Hands should be in front of the ball.

The grip end of the shaft should lean toward the target.

Your weight should favor the front foot (60 percent left, 40 percent right).

Your nose should be in front of the ball.

Maintain a slightly open stance (a line drawn across your toes would point farther to the left of your target than parallel).

Choke down on the club a bit, so that 1 or 2" (2.5 to 5cm) of the grip is visible above your hands.

A slightly open clubface will help to glide through the turf without "grabbing."

Key Positions of the Swing

Begin the Backswing

Taking the proper address position is critical for effective chipping. Your right shoulder should be slightly lower than the left, but your weight is shifted to the left, so the shoulders appear nearly level with the horizon. (Note that the spine angle is nearly vertical from this perspective.) Keep your left arm long and relaxed, and use a medium grip pressure to allow the club to move comfortably without stiffening the arms.

Completion of the Backswing

Since the chip is a smaller swing, you don't need to take the club back too far for the backswing—for most chips, the clubhead won't swing higher than your knees. Using your shoulders, rock the club back (notice the "Y" at address simply rotates). Keep the club shaft in line with the left forearm. Your left arm moves back at the same pace as the club—a "one-piece" take-away. Don't hinge the wrists. Throughout the entire backswing keep your lower body still (don't turn your hips), and your weight on the left side. The club does not stay on the target line; it will move to the inside during the backswing.

Downswing and Impact

As you come down to impact, begin to gently rotate your hips toward the target. Keep the left arm long and relaxed—resist the temptation to "lift" the ball or help it into the air. The loft of the clubface will do all the work. It's very important to have your hands ahead of the ball prior to impact for a smooth, sweeping motion. Although the chip is a slightly descending blow that will brush the turf in front of the ball, you should not create a divot. Keep your eyes on the ball.

Finish

The finish is similar in length to the backswing—the clubhead finishes below the knees. Because your weight has remained on the left side throughout the entire chipping motion, you should feel very stable over your left foot. The "Y" has now rotated to the finish. Be sure to maintain that straight line formed by the club shaft and the left forearm, and don't unhinge your wrists. Rotate your head toward the target so that you can watch the ball roll.

Swing Sequence (Front)

Here is how the entire swing should look from the front:

Remember to keep the chip swing small.

Keep your weight forward (on the left side), hands forward, and a ball position behind center.

Don't hinge your wrists.

Keep your left arm long and relaxed.

Your weight remains on the left (forward) side.

Swing Sequence (Side)

Here is how the entire swing should look from the side:

Keep your eyes focused on the ball at impact.

Hips rotate gently toward the target.

The back of your wrist stays flat and square with the left forearm through impact—no "flipping."

Keep a smooth tempo from backswing to follow-through. Don't "chop" or stop at the ball. The clubhead should continue through impact to a balanced finish.

Additional Considerations

Reading the Break

A chip shot is designed to keep the ball low and have it roll a significant distance on the green. Since the chip spends a long time rolling, it's important to assess the contour of the green before choosing a target line. As with putting, slope and gravity will cause a chipped ball to roll at different speeds and in different directions. Take that into account before choosing your target line; you might have to aim away from the hole in order to knock it close.

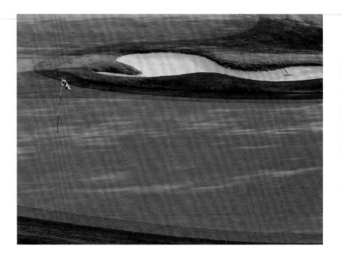

Chipping from the Rough

Most chip shots take place from the fringe or fairway surrounding a green. But you can also chip from the taller grass. There are two keys for chipping from the rough. First, it's important to have a very good lie. If the ball has settled down too deeply, you will need to make a bigger swing with more of a wrist hinge. Second, since grass is likely to get trapped between the clubface and the ball, the ball is likely to "squirt" forward with very little spin. A ball chipped cleanly from the rough is likely to roll farther than a chip from short grass. Be sure to calculate for the extra roll.

Chipping with Different Clubs

Although most opt for an 8- or 9-iron, a chip shot can be made with a variety of clubs. Once you've mastered the basics of the chipping stroke, you can change your club selection to change the results. A chip with a sand wedge may clear the fringe and stop after a short roll, whereas that same chip with a 7-iron would land with less spin and more forward momentum, and would roll much farther. Practice chipping with different clubs and you'll develop a better feel for shots around the green.

Chipping with Hybrids

I've discussed chipping with different irons, but there's also another option: chipping with a hybrid or a fairway wood. Chipping with a hybrid has some advantages. The sole of the hybrid is wider than the sole of an iron, and will glide across the turf nicely. The ball should be positioned closer to the middle of the stance to chip with a hybrid, and the motion should mimic a putting stroke. This technique is especially useful if your ball is in a divot or a very tight lie near the green. Practice the hybrid chip—you may find it to be a very useful option.

Common Mistakes

Below are two common chipping mistakes, along with corrections that will lead to success.

Flipping

Since chipping takes place so close to the green, many players are reluctant to accelerate through the ball to a comfortable finish. Their arms slow down, and they unhinge their wrists during or just prior to impact. This "flipping" motion leads to poor contact and inconsistent results.

One key to solid chipping is to keep the left wrist in a straight line with the left forearm through impact, as shown. The hands actually pass the ball before the club makes contact with the ball. Unlike the flip or a lift, this sweeping motion leads to clean contact.

All Arms, No Hips

Since chipping is a smaller motion, many golfers forget to turn their body through to the finish, and only use their arms for the chip. This is what it looks like when you use an "all arms" chip. Using only your arms will result in a very awkward and very mechanical move, and you'll hit the ball near the equator—which will propel the ball past the cup and across the green.

When you use your whole body and turn your hips, as you see here, it will be easier to keep your hands in front of the ball at impact. Turning the hips to the finish also relaxes the hands, leading to more consistent results.

Picture This!

The Broom

A great chip looks like a sweeping motion, so this broom image is perfect to keep in mind! If you sweep dust on the floor, your weight is forward, the broomstick leans forward, and your hands are in front of the bristles. That same motion works for chipping. Keep this broom image in mind, and you'll master the chip shot!

The Rifle

Although they barely move during the backswing, the hips should rotate gently toward the target during the forward motion of a chip. If your hips stay motionless and you use only your arms, you're more likely to unhinge (flip) your wrists through impact. After a wristy chip, you'll notice the grip end of the club points back at your midsection. Imagine that instead of a club you're holding the barrel of a rifle. If you turn your hips through the chip, it's much easier to lead the barrel safely past your body. No hips and a flip of the wrists, and that barrel is pointing straight at you!

Practice Drill 1: The Butter Knife

"Flipping" or unhinging the left wrist during a chip shot can lead to poor results. This drill can help you feel the proper wrist positions for chipping.

Simply slide a butter knife under your watch strap. The knife will act as a splint and keep your left wrist square and in line with your left forearm through impact to the finish.

Practice by making some rehearsal strokes first. Get used to feeling the proper position as you brush the turf. Then address a ball and repeat the motion. Of course, be sure to use a dull butter knife—a mistake with a sharp steak knife could be very painful!

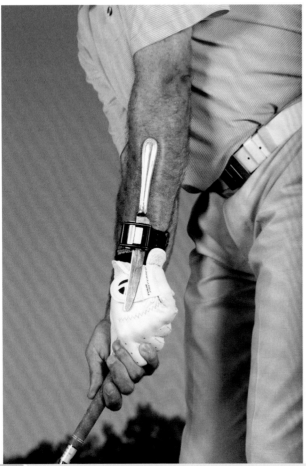
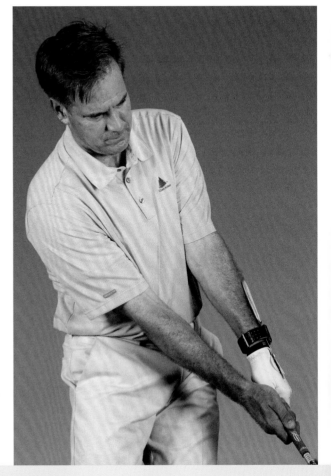

Practice Drill 2: Towel Under the Foot

For a great chip shot, your weight should be favoring the left side at address, and stay there during the backswing. The towel drill can help to keep your weight on the left side throughout the chipping motion.

Roll up a golf towel and wedge it under the outside of your right foot. Once the towel is in place, take some practice chipping swings. The towel will assist you in keeping your weight to the left. As you finish the shot, allow your weight to transfer even more to the left as your hips rotate toward the target.

Once you're comfortable with the sensation of keeping your weight on the left side, hit a few chip shots with the towel in place.

pitching

Although not a full swing, a pitch requires more motion and clubhead speed than a chip shot. The pitch shot typically flies higher and farther in the air than a chip, and doesn't roll nearly as far once it hits the green. This shot is made with your most lofted clubs (pitching wedge, cap wedge, sand wedge, or lob wedge), which cause the ball to spin more and launch with a higher trajectory. As a result, the ball lands softly and stops quickly on the putting surface. The ball spins more and stops quicker when this shot is played from the fairway, but the pitch is also very useful from the greenside rough and for those instances when you need to lob your ball over a bunker. The pitch is not exclusive to greenside situations—there are times when you may need to "take your medicine" and pitch out to the fairway from behind a tree or from heavy rough.

If you need to launch your ball up in the air and stop it quickly, the pitch is the shot for you. Learning the basics of pitching will help you lower your scores!

The Setup

front

side

Your feet should be wider than they are during a chip shot—approximately shoulder width.

Weight should be a touch left, but closer to 50/50.

The ball should be in the center of your stance.

Hands should be just a touch in front of the ball.

Nose should be right above the ball.

Stance should be slightly open (feet, knees, and hips aligned slightly left of target line).

Use the standard grip position, but for shorter shots, choke down a bit for better control.

The left arm should be long and both arms should feel relaxed.

Don't crowd the ball, and leave some space between hands and thighs.

Key Positions of the Swing

Begin the Backswing

Keeping your weight balanced between both feet, begin to turn. Your weight should not shift to the right side. Don't try to keep the clubface "looking" at the ball; it should rotate open naturally. As the club rotates open, start to hinge your wrist (this adds clubhead speed). Be careful not to "drag" the handle away from the ball during this first move. The club shaft should be at a higher angle already, indicating the start of the hinge.

Completion of the Backswing

Rotate your shoulders, keeping the left arm long. Your weight stays centered, and you should feel pressure on the instep of your right foot—*not* on the outside of that foot. At this point the wrist hinge is complete, and your right elbow should not be higher than your left. If you make a comfortable shoulder turn, that right elbow should be close to your body. Your hips should rotate just a touch.

Downswing and Impact

As you come down for impact, your hips should begin a more obvious rotation toward the target; your weight should now be favoring the left side. Your relaxed arms begin to drop as the hips begin to rotate forward. At impact your belt buckle should be pointing in front of the ball. Keep your eyes focused on the ball, your nose positioned over it, and your hands slightly in front of it. Keep your left arm long and your grip pressure consistent through the entire motion.

Finish

Keep your acceleration going through impact—don't chop or stop your swing just after you hit the ball. Move the club smoothly from backswing to follow-through. The length of the finish should at least match the length of the backswing. You should still have some spine tilt at this point; your weight should be largely on the left side, and your right heel should have lifted off the ground a bit. Chest and belt buckle should be pointing toward the target.

Swing Sequence (Front)

Here is how the entire swing should look from the front:

Leave space under your chin to allow for a smooth shoulder turn throughout.

Notice the centered backswing.

Be sure your weight does not shift to the right side.

Note the hinge in your wrist.

Keep your left arm long and your nose over the ball.

Keep your hips relatively "quiet"—don't turn them nearly as much as the shoulders.

Swing Sequence (Side)

Here is how the entire swing should look from the side:

Don't rush: keep a steady tempo and smooth acceleration from backswing through impact.

The hinge angle is still in place.

Hips have rotated past the ball and weight is moving farther to the left side.

Eyes should be focused on the ball.

Maintain your height from address and a long left arm.

Hands should be a bit in front of the ball.

Keep your arms moving to achieve a nice extension. If the arms stop near impact, the wrists will unhinge and release the club too early.

Resist the temptation to stand up through the shot.

The weight is now on the left side, and there is air under the right heel. A relaxed, balanced finish is important.

Additional Considerations

Tempo

Great pitching requires great tempo. The rhythm of your swing is very important in golf, and poor rhythm shows up very quickly in a pitch shot. Any sudden speed changes during your swing will have negative results. A smooth backswing should transition into smooth acceleration to the finish; do not rush down to the ball, or stop just after impact. Length of follow-through should mirror length of backswing, and the motion should be smooth and finish with balance.

Assess the Lie and Adjust the Swing

In golf, conditions can change dramatically from shot to shot. When pitching, it's important to carefully assess the lie of your ball. Although the basic mechanics of the swing are the same, you need to adjust your settings based on how heavy the grass is and how deep the ball has settled. When you have a lot of grass to cut through, you need to open the clubface slightly, increase grip pressure a bit and increase the length of your backswing. Deeper grass requires a longer backswing!

Swinging Uphill

You'll find that many putting surfaces on a golf course are elevated. If you miss a green, it's not uncommon to be faced with an uphill pitch shot. In these cases, you need to resist the temptation to stand vertical with the horizon (below left). That setup leads to a "chop," where the club enters the ground at a very steep angle. In these situations, you need to tilt your spine away from the target and set up with your shoulders nearly matching the ground line (below right). This allows you to swing through the shot without striking the ground abruptly. This tip isn't limited to just pitching—keep this in mind with any uphill shot you may face on the golf course.

Common Mistakes

Pitching is a very useful shot to have in your arsenal, but you need to practice this shot to avoid some bad habits.

Below, I've highlighted two common pitching flaws along with corrections to keep you on the right track.

Big Backswing, Short Follow-Through

Many golfers have a pitching backswing that's much longer than they realize. If the backswing is too long, then smooth acceleration through impact will carry the ball too far. Most golfers try to slow down at impact to prevent the ball from going too far. "Slowing down" at impact leads to very inconsistent results.

Decreasing the length of your backswing will allow you to accelerate through impact without launching the ball too far. Try taking a smaller backswing and then smoothly gather speed through impact. Your pitches will be cleaner and you'll begin gauging distances better.

The Steep Chop

When you're close to the green, it's easy to lose sight of proper swing plane. Golfers who only need to move the ball a short distance tend to lift the club up quickly and chop down steeply. This very vertical path leads to "topping" the ball, or digging the club into the ground before contact.

Although the pitch can be a smaller swing, it's important to remember that this is a small version of the normal swing. A good pitching motion will move the club on a tilted plane that matches that of the club shaft at address. The club should swing back to the inside as shown, then through impact on that same tilted plane for best results.

Picture This!

Swinging in a Barrel

It's easy to get a little sloppy with your swing from time to time. For crisp, clean pitches, imagine that you're swinging in a barrel. This time-tested image helps to eliminate the sliding, lateral movement that leads to poor contact. The barrel image will help you turn effectively and keep your swing stable and centered.

Targeting the Landing Spot

With every golf shot, it's important to have a clear picture of how you want your ball to travel. After assessing your lie and judging the slopes on the green, decide on the best "flight pattern" for your shot. Pick your target carefully! It's often helpful to "let go" of the flag and focus clearly on the landing spot that will lead you to the best results.

Practice Drill 1: The Cookie Drill

In this pitching section we've discussed the importance of finding a nice tempo and rhythm to your swing. The cookie drill is a great exercise to help you stay relaxed and begin to feel the smooth balance of a successful pitch shot.

Take a cookie (a crisp, crunchy cookie is best) and place it between your teeth. Then pick up a wedge and make some smooth, balanced practice swings. Then, while keeping the cookie in place, address a ball and take a shot. If you tense up or change speeds violently, the cookie is very likely to get crunched. If you can keep the cookie from breaking, you're staying more relaxed during the shot. Better rhythm and better results are sure to follow!

Practice Drill 2: Swinging Under the Foam

Many golfers who are uncomfortable pitching the ball will lift the club too quickly and descend on the ball in a very vertical fashion. That steep chopping motion leads to poor contact and a total lack of distance control. This swing plane drill will help to keep your club moving in the right direction.

Many stores carry these foam tubes that kids love to use in swimming pools, or you could also use pipe insulation tubes available at any hardware store. After finding some foam and an alignment rod, take your pitching address position with a wedge. Then stick the alignment rod in the ground on an angle that matches the angle of your club shaft at address. Slide the foam over the alignment rod and make some practice swings that pass comfortably under the foam. If you swing too quick or too steep, you're likely to strike the foam. Feel the club swinging around you on the tilted plane defined by the foam, and ultimately hit some shots from this same station. This drill will keep you from getting too vertical on these little shots—and you'll make better contact!

bunker shots

Everyone loves a trip to the beach, right? Well, finding the sand on a golf course is not quite as fun, until you learn the basics of a bunker shot.

Golf is far more than teeing grounds, fairways, and greens. Most golf courses feature boundary lines, heavy rough, wooded areas, and various bodies of water, all designed to punish and challenge you should you hit a ball in the wrong place. Of all the hazards on a golf course, the sand bunker seems to get the most attention. Many greens are guarded by bunkers, and when you hit a wayward approach that misses the putting surface, your next swing is often from the sand. Bunkers come in various shapes and sizes. In addition to greenside sand, there are also fairway bunkers that will gobble up misguided tee shots on par 4s and par 5s.

Escaping a greenside bunker is easiest with your most lofted clubs—the pitching wedge (PW), sand wedge (SW), and lob wedge (LW). The swing is similar to the pitch shot motion, but will often require a longer backswing and a longer follow-through. In fairway bunkers, you should make contact with the ball first, but the greenside bunker shot is much different. It's the only shot in golf where you intentionally hit the ground *before* the ball. The club enters the sand a couple of inches behind the ball, and as the swing continues forward, the sand is displaced and actually "splashes" the ball out onto the green. Learning this specialty shot will help you avoid a big score from a sandy hazard.

The Setup

front

side

Take a firm stance with your feet at least shoulder-width apart.

Your weight should be just slightly forward (55 percent on the left side).

The ball should be forward of center.

Hands should be positioned slightly behind the ball.

Club should be gripped so that the face is open (facing slightly to the right of your swing path).

Stance should be open—a line drawn across your toes should aim to the left of your target.

Feet should shimmy down into the sand a bit for stability.

Maintain a comfortable knee flex.

Key Positions of the Swing

Begin the Backswing

Having the proper address position is critical for greenside bunker shots. Be sure to take your grip so that the clubface is "open." Then aim farther to the left than you would on a standard iron shot. Grip pressure should be firm, but not too tight: your wrists need to hinge smoothly for this shot. Keep a comfortable, normal spine angle and some space under your chin; don't bend any more from the waist than normal.

Top of the Backswing

A good shot from the sand requires significant club-head speed, which comes from a nice wrist hinge as shown. Be careful not to shift your weight to the right; you should still be favoring your left side. Due to the open clubface and the need to splash through sand, your backswing should be longer than that of a pitch shot from the same distance. Notice the left arm remains fully extended.

Downswing and Impact

This is where the bunker swing differs from a standard wedge shot. Initial contact with the ground should take place 1" (2.5cm) to 3" (7.5cm) behind the ball (with soft, fluffy sand, the entry point can be 3" behind the ball; if the sand is wet or compact, the club should enter the sand closer to the ball). Since the ball is forward in your stance and your feet have dug below the surface a bit, the club should enter the sand first, sweeping under the ball, and splashing it onto the green. Maintain your height—resist the temptation to lower yourself during this swing.

Finish

Your weight will favor the left side during the entire swing, but now should be visibly closer to the target. Don't chop, dig, or stop at the ball. It's important to accelerate through the sand to this finish position; if you don't have enough speed to splash sand out of the bunker, then the ball won't make it out either. The clubface should not rotate as much as it would during a shot from the fairway. Due to the "open" position of the face at address, and the swing path to the left, the clubface should stay "open" longer through impact.

Swing Sequence (Front)

Here is how the entire swing should look from the front:

A rule in golf states that when in a bunker, you cannot "ground" your club (touch sand with your club) at address or during the take-away. You certainly want to splash sand on the downswing, but hover your club above the sand at address!

Wrist hinge is necessary for a successful bunker shot. You can see the hinge taking place early in the backswing.

Not much hip rotation, but the shoulders have made a pretty good turn—which is essential to create effective clubhead speed. Weight has not shifted to the right side.

Swing Sequence (Side)

Here is how the entire swing should look from the side:

The left arm is long, and the key here is that the hands are directly above or even slightly behind the ball at impact. That ensures a splash and not a dig.

Maintain the speed through impact to the finish. Arms should extend freely as shown. You should be balanced and your weight should be on your left side.

Arms should extend freely as shown. You should be balanced and your weight should be on your left side.

If you watch the pros on TV, you'll notice when they enter a bunker, they "shimmy" their feet into the sand. There are two reasons they do this: first, they are creating a stable footing for their shot; second, they are testing the sand to see whether it's firm or fluffy.

Additional Considerations

Uphill and Downhill Lies

When your ball bounces into a bunker, it usually rolls down to a relatively flat lie—but not always. The important thing to remember when you have an uphill or downhill lie in the bunker is to keep your shoulders parallel with the slope. If your shoulders stay parallel with the horizon, you're likely to get poor results from these uneven lies. Also remember that an uphill shot will fly higher and stop quicker. A shot from a downhill lie will fly lower and roll farther. Be sure to calculate for those distance-altering factors.

Bounce

Just because you're in the sand, don't feel obligated to use the sand wedge. For higher, shorter shots you could try a lob wedge, and for longer shots a pitching wedge could come in handy. The main thing to consider is "bounce." Bounce refers to the angle of a club's sole or bottom. In soft or fluffy sand conditions, it's helpful to have more bounce (12, 14, or 16 degrees). From tight lies or hard, wet sand, it's better to have less bounce (6 or 8 degrees). Most wedges indicate the degrees of bounce in addition to degrees of loft. Make sure you have the right bounce for your course conditions.

The "Fried Egg"

I love fried eggs for breakfast, but I hate them on a golf course. In golf, a "fried egg" describes a very bad lie in the bunker. It occurs when a ball flies straight into the sand and plugs. A portion of the ball is actually buried below the surface, making the ball look a bit like a fried egg. With part of the ball submerged, this can be a much more difficult shot—unless you know the keys to success. In this case, an open clubface won't usually work. You need to square the face and allow your club to dig under the buried ball. Make your normal bunker swing, but with a little extra speed. The square face will dig the ball out onto the green. Be prepared for the ball to come out on a lower trajectory and roll farther on the green than a normal sand shot.

Additional Considerations

Escaping Fairway Bunkers

With greenside bunker shots, a high-lofted club hits the bunker first and splashes the ball out by displacing the sand underneath the ball. Fairway bunker shots are significantly different. These fairway bunkers are designed to catch wayward shots from the tee on par 4s and par 5s, and lay-up shots. Most common on par 5s, the lay-up is a position shot played when the golfer does not feel comfortable trying to reach the green in two. The golfer hits this safer, shorter shot that's designed to give a nicer position to approach the green on their next shot. Many courses position fairway bunkers near the most ideal "lay-up" zones; a miscalculation in shot distance or direction leads to a ball in the sand. Fairway bunkers are located much farther from the green, and typically are more level, without the high lips and edges of a greenside bunker.

During a swing from a fairway bunker, the club strikes the ball *before* striking the sand. The shot is actually very similar to a typical shot from the middle of the fairway, and you can use a wide variety of clubs—even longer irons and/or hybrid clubs if the forward edge or front lip of the bunker is low enough. Important hints for hitting a clean fairway bunker shot:

- Place the ball closer to the middle of your stance.

- In sand you will not be able to brace yourself firmly for a full swing. So because your stance is less stable, take one club stronger (for example: a 6-iron instead of a 7-iron) and swing smoothly.

- Don't dig or swing down too sharply—the idea is to sweep this shot, making sure to strike the ball before striking the sand with your club.

Common Mistakes

Here are two common flaws to be wary of as you work on your bunker swing. Practicing the proper positions that accompany them will be time well spent.

The Shimmy

Getting a firm footing in the sand is recommended, but if you shimmy too far down into the sand, you're likely to hit too far behind the ball. If the sand is very soft, and you need to get deeper footing than normal, be sure to choke down on the grip of your club to avoid "digging" with your swing.

Do a minimal amount of wiggling with your feet to create a stable address. This photo shows my feet in a strong position without digging too far below the surface.

The Dig

This is the look of a golfer who is determined to excavate his ball from the bunker. The ball is too far back, the swing is far too vertical, his nose is in front of the ball, and he's about to bury his club deep into the sand. The problem? This ball has no chance of being splashed onto the green.

Maintain height, position your nose behind the ball, and think of splashing sand out of the bunker. From this proper position, the club will enter the sand, pass under the ball, and propel it onto the putting surface. You won't bury the club deep; you'll hear a nice "thump" as the sand (and the ball) splash out smoothly.

Picture This!

Splash!

It's no mistake that I've referred to the bunker shot numerous times as a "splash." Imagine the motion of splashing a bug out of a pool with your hand. You need to get under the bug, but stay shallow enough to launch him (and the water under him) out of the pool. Think of the angle that the palm of your hand would make where your hand would enter the water: that motion is exactly like a bunker shot. I combined that thought with a sand wedge and a plastic ball to give you this helpful splash image!

The Cup

During a successful bunker shot, the face of your wedge will stay open longer than it would during a typical shot from the turf. Many of my students have improved their bunker results by imagining that their clubface "looks to the sky" after impact. This image takes that idea a step further. By visualizing a cup of water balancing on your clubface at this point during the swing, your shots will fly higher and land softer.

Practice Drill 1: Lines in the Sand

This is my favorite bunker shot drill. Draw two lines in the sand perpendicular to your target line—one that represents where the ball would be, and then another parallel line approximately 3 inches (7.5cm) behind the ball line. After setting up and addressing the ball line, take a practice swing with the intent to enter the sand on the back line. Now take a look at the splash mark (divot) you made. A successful divot will start on or very near the back line and exit the sand a few inches in front of the ball line, and the divot should be relatively shallow. After a few practice swings, substitute a ball for the front line. Practice this drill often. If you can consistently control your entry point, you'll become a great bunker player.

Practice Drill 2: Sand on the Face

This drill can help you feel the sensation of quiet hands and less rotation through impact. Remember, as you pass through impact, your hands should be relatively "quiet"—they shouldn't rotate as quickly and naturally as they would during a regular swing. Quick hand rotation can lead to a closed clubface, which is not ideal for sand shots. Take your address position. Instead of taking a backswing, simply scoop a little sand onto the face of your wedge and slowly continue through the impact area to the position shown. Keeping the sand on your clubface at this point will help you to understand how the hands move through impact. If you dump the sand, you're using too much rotation.

on the green

Powerful drives and towering iron shots bring joy to every golfer, but whether you're on the PGA Tour or on your local mini-golf course, the player who putts the best usually brings home the money! Of the fourteen clubs allowed in golf, none are used more than the putter—yet most golfers spend nearly *all* of their practice time working on full swings. Never underestimate the importance of putting!

The following pages will teach you how to prepare for and execute a consistent and effective putting stroke. You'll also learn speed control and some critical green-reading skills that will help you judge the direction your ball is likely to travel. Let's roll!

putting

Putters have very little loft, and are designed to roll a golf ball along the putting surface toward the hole. Although it's permissible (and sometimes wise) to putt from the surrounding fringe, the putter is typically used once your ball is on the green. No single golf club comes in more shapes and sizes. Some are long and some are short, and the differences in grip size and clubhead design are vast. But the basic, successful putting stroke has very specific characteristics, regardless of club design.

The Setup

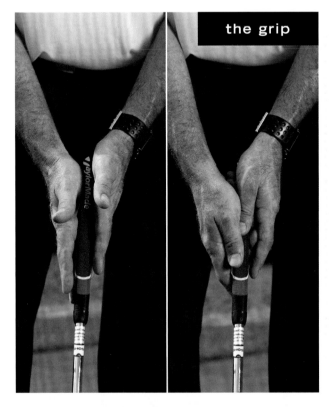

the grip

Putter grip should be positioned more in the palms than the fingers.

Palms should face each other.

Palms should match the position of the putter face.

Both thumbs should rest on the front, flat side of the grip.

Grip pressure should be relatively light, but consistent throughout the stroke.

the stance

Feet should be slightly less than shoulder-width apart.

Feet and shoulders should be parallel with target line.

Maintain comfortable knee flex and spine angle.

The weight should be evenly distributed, 50/50.

Your eyes should be positioned directly over the ball.

Your left shoulder is only slightly higher than the right.

The ball is positioned just forward of center.

Arms hang naturally, and hands should be even with the ball.

The putter shaft should be in line with forearms.

Grips

A variety of gripping styles and techniques have emerged over the years, primarily because of an affliction known as the "yips"—an involuntary muscle spasm in the hands or wrists that takes place during the putting stroke. That little spasm causes many putts to miss. Players have created a number of different grips and techniques to limit the negative impact of the yip. If the standard style of putting grip is not working for you, try one of these alternative methods.

Left Hand Low: This grip style, which is also known as putting "cross-handed," is achieved by switching the positions of your hands on the putter grip. By placing the left hand on the low side, the left shoulder also drops a bit, making the shoulder line nearly parallel with the horizon. This grip tends to stabilize the left hand and keep the putter face very square through impact.

The Claw: With this style, the left hand is applied to the club in a very traditional fashion, but the fingers of the right hand are positioned much differently. Separate the index and middle finger from the ring finger and pinkie. Then "split" the club by curling two fingers on the top of the grip and two fingers below, as shown. This grip effectively eliminates any involvement from the fingers on your right hand.

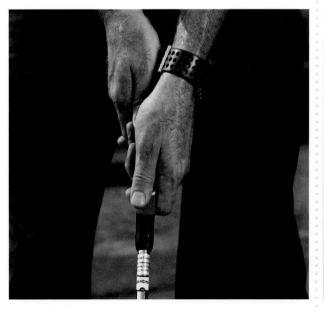

The Saw: Similar to the claw, this grip diminishes the use of the right hand. The left hand holds the club in a traditional manner, but the right hand is flipped to the top side of the shaft and positioned as shown. The thumb is gently placed under the grip, while the fingers are outstretched and side by side on top. The right forearm will come away from the body and align with the fingers, pointing down the target line. With this positioning of the right arm and fingers, the stroke looks similar to a sawing motion.

The Splint: This may look severe, but it's actually a very effective grip. The left hand reaches way down to the bottom of the grip and the right hand then grabs the left forearm just below the elbow. With the end of the grip now locked into place by the right hand, the putter will almost feel like a splint or a cast on your left forearm. This grip will instantly remind you that your shoulders are very important in the putting stroke. Just rock the shoulders and the putter, wrists, and hands are all locked in position. This style was made very popular by Masters Champion Bernhard Langer.

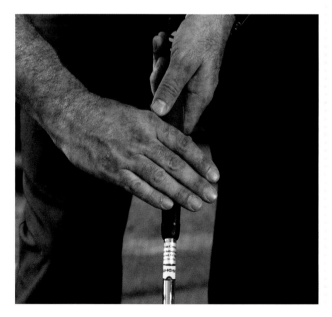
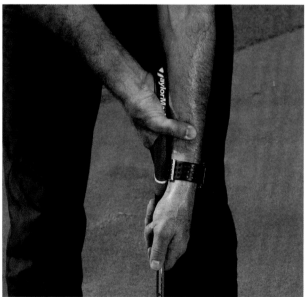

Key Positions of the Stroke

Begin the Backswing

Although your nose is slightly behind the ball, the club shaft should be at least vertical, if not leaning toward the target a touch. Your hands should be even with the ball. It's helpful to visualize the triangle that's formed between your shoulders and your grip.

Completion of the Backswing

Rotate the shoulders gently to swing the putter back in a smooth, pendulum-like motion. The "triangle" formation at address is still intact. Keep your weight centered and focus clearly on the ball. Your head should be perfectly still, your hands and wrists very quiet, and there should be no movement below the belt. Keep the putter low to the ground so that you're not lifting or hinging during the backswing.

Downswing and Impact

Rock the shoulders to bring the putter head back through impact toward the finish. At impact, the hands should return to the position they were in at address. The triangle shape stays consistent and the hands remain quiet—no unhinging or flipping at the ball. Your hands should work as a team—one should not overpower the other, and grip pressure should remain consistent. Eyes stay focused on the ball, and the head should not move from its position at address. The putter should swing above the putting surface— it should *not* make contact with the ground during the stroke.

Finish

The follow-through of a putting stroke is very important. A smooth, balanced stroke gently gathers speed and swings through the ball to the finish position shown. A good follow-through should be nearly as long as the backswing if you're putting with good tempo. Your focus should not leave the spot on the ground where the ball was. Keeping a still head like this assures better contact. Don't look toward the hole until the ball has been struck and has rolled a couple feet from its original position; then slowly swivel your head and watch the results. Left shoulder higher than the right equals a good follow-through.

The Putting Routine

Once your ball lands on the green, there's a fairly consistent process to follow:

1. Mark your ball with a coin or a ball marker (just behind the ball, opposite from the hole).

2. Repair the mark that your ball may have made in the putting surface.

3. Remove your glove (many prefer to putt without a glove for greater feel).

4. "Read" the green and decide how the ball might curve on its way to the hole.

5. Choose your target line.

6. When it's your turn to putt, replace your ball (using the line drawn if you choose) and remove the ball marker.

7. Take a practice swing or two and decide on the speed needed.

8. Address the ball, take one last look at the target, and make a confident stroke.

Additional Considerations

Speed

After determining the break, the next consideration is speed. How much do you need to roll the ball comfortably into the cup, without rolling it too far past the hole should you miss? Putts made in the direction the grass is growing will have more speed than putts made "against the grain." If it starts to rain, or a green has recently been watered, the speed of the green will slow down considerably. And obviously an uphill putt will be slower than a downhill putt. It's important to predict these factors and adjust the length of your putting stroke accordingly. The longer the back and through swing, the more speed and roll you will create.

The Break

Putting greens can have significant slopes and undulations that will cause your ball to veer ("break") to the left or the right. You have to "read the green" (predict the ball's movement) by looking at the ground surrounding the green. Putts tend to break away from the higher side. Imagine tipping over a huge drum of water toward the hole. If you can envision where the water would flow, you can read a green successfully!

Lining Up the Ball

Visualize the line your ball will take toward the hole by picking out a spot (maybe an imperfection or discoloration in the green) along that imaginary line, a couple inches in front of your ball marker. Draw a straight line on your ball (you can eyeball it, or use a device like the one shown in the picture), and place the ball with the line pointing directly at the spot you picked out. Set your putter face perpendicular to the line, and make your stroke.

Common Mistakes

You've learned the proper mechanics of the putting stroke, and I encourage you to practice often. Highlighted below are two common putting flaws. Practicing with proper technique will quickly pay off!

Peeking

wrong

Peeking is very common, especially during relatively short putts. There is often a very strong desire to watch the ball as it leaves the putter face. Players might even anticipate where the ball is going to roll, and begin to turn their head toward the target prior to impact. The early look (peek) usually indicates a lack of confidence, and leads to poor contact and missed putts.

right

Before making your stroke, imagine there's a dot or a ball marker under your ball. After making your stroke, your focus should initially remain on that spot where the ball was at address. After the ball has rolled a couple feet, you should gently swivel your head to follow its path. But keeping your gaze steady and on that spot through impact will lead to better contact, better distance control, and more putts made.

Losing the Flat Left Wrist Through Impact

A common problem in putting occurs when the arms slow or stop during the stroke and the hands unhinge through impact. This error is evident when the angle between the putter shaft and the left forearm increases dramatically. This change in angle during the stroke leads to poor results.

Note the angle between your left forearm and the putter shaft at address. That angle should remain the same throughout the entire putting stroke. It will feel as though your hands are less involved and the back of your left wrist is moving squarely and firmly through the ball. Keeping the address position consistent through impact leads to lower scores.

Picture This!

The CD

A solid address position will help you to become a great putter. Ideally, your eyes should be positioned directly above the ball before making your putting stroke—but how would you know? Well, dropping a CD on the ground (shiny side up) and placing a ball in the center is step one. Then address the ball, and look for the reflection of your eyes in the CD. If you can see your eyes even with (or just to the inside of) the ball, then you are positioned properly.

The Steve Martin

Yes, Steve Martin can make you a better putter. Keeping your eyes level through the putting stroke leads to solid contact and great distance control. Some putters "rock" their head and eye-line back during the take-away (picture 1), then reverse that motion on the way through (picture 2). That rocking motion leads to trouble on the putting green. Imagine you're wearing Martin's arrow through the head. Keep that arrow level throughout the stroke and you'll make more putts!

Practice Drill 1: The Wire Hanger

This is a great way to practice keeping your head steady throughout the stroke. Take a wire clothes hanger, fashion a circle in one end, and insert the other end in the putting green on an angle. After placing a ball directly under the circle, address the ball so that you can see it centered below the circle as shown. As you take the putter away, the ball should still appear perfectly centered, and should remain visually centered in the circle through impact. If the ball drifts out of the circle at any point, your head is moving! Keep practicing until the ball appears centered throughout your motion.

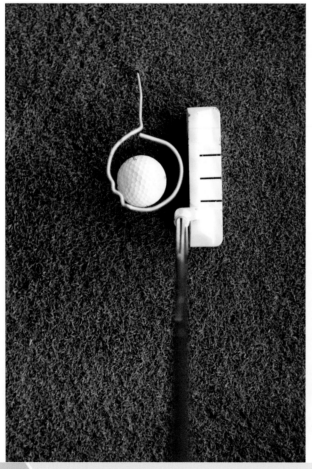

Practice Drill 2: Throwing in the Towels

Here's a simple and very effective way to work on your distance control. Take one, two, or three small towels—approximately 14" × 20" (35cm × 50cm)—and place them on the green at different distances: 5' (1.5m), 10' (3m), and 15' (4.5m) away. Practice rolling putts with the goal of keeping your golf balls on the chosen towel. When you feel confident at 5', move to the 10' towel, and then try the 15' towel. Switch towel targets periodically, and challenge yourself with different games and point systems—it's critical to make your practice session fun as well as challenging! When you go out to the course, visualize the towel behind the cup. This drill can even be done on your living room carpet (although I don't recommend practicing on a shag rug).

trouble shots

Many new golfers are introduced to the game on the driving range—and frankly, that's an excellent approach. Learning and practicing at the range allows you to work on the basics without any concerns about other players in your group or the various rules and regulations that apply at an actual golf course. But as a PGA instructor, I can assure you that the game becomes a bit more challenging once you tee it up for your first official round of golf. I've been teaching golf for decades, and one comment I hear frequently from beginners is: "I hit the ball great on the driving range, but I can't seem to swing as well on the course."

There are a number of reasons why the golf course is more challenging. For starters, the mood at the practice range always seems more casual. Nobody keeps score, you can take as many swings as you like, there isn't as much time between shots, and there's a general lack of pressure. In addition to that significant lack of tension, there are no trees, bunkers, or water to interfere with your swing. At the range, every swing is from perfectly level ground and from a perfect lie; conditions are much different on an actual course.

But fear not! The challenges you should expect when playing golf are part of the true enjoyment of this game. Overcoming obstacles makes golf exciting, and gives us plenty to talk about after the round. I will discuss some helpful psychological strategies later in the book, but this chapter is dedicated to trouble shot technique. The following pages will show you how to manage difficult conditions you're likely to encounter on the course.

escaping the rough

Tees, fairways, and greens are beautiful places to play from. The rough? … not so much. Rough is the deeper, thicker grass that lies beyond the optimal landing spots. If you miss your target, your ball is likely to come to rest in this longer, heavier grass. Thick rough will typically slow down your club and make it difficult to advance the ball as far as you would expect. Rough also tends to wrap around the hosel or neck of the club and "close" the clubface prior to impact, which causes many players to miss to the left. Rough will also decrease the amount of spin your club applies to the ball, which will make it difficult to stop the ball on the green.

Although this all sounds rather frustrating, there's a very helpful process for dealing with this situation. Follow these steps, and you will escape the rough without too much concern.

1. **Assess the lie:** not all rough is created equal. If your ball has nestled down deep into heavy rough, your options are limited. If near the green, you can probably loft the ball onto the putting surface; if you're much farther from the hole, "take your medicine" and lay up! Grab your highest lofted club and plan on advancing the ball to the nearest fairway condition, so you can then swing freely toward your ultimate target. If the lie is a little better, and you can see most of the ball, you might choose a 9-, 8-, or even a 7-iron. If you're lucky and get a great lie where very little grass is going to be trapped between the clubface and the ball when you swing, then you can get more aggressive and expect reasonably normal distance from your irons or even a hybrid club. But remember, the ball will roll farther after it lands than it would after a swing from the fairway.

2. From rough, it helps to **open your stance** a touch. Rather than setting up perfectly parallel to your target, aim your feet a few degrees to the left.

3. Now that you're aiming just a bit to the left, you should **open the face of your club** before gripping it. If the clubface is open a bit, it cuts through heavy grass better, which will help to make better contact with the ball.

4. **Increase your grip pressure.** Earlier in this book I recommended grip pressure of 6 on a scale of 0 to 10. From the rough, you should increase to 7 or 8 so that you can maintain control of the club as it travels through thick grass.

5. **Resist the temptation to "chop"** and stop at the ball. With the adjustments listed, you're ready to make a full swing. Yes, the rough may slow down your speed through impact, but you must commit to the shot and plan on swinging to a full finish.

uneven lies

Unlike driving ranges, golf courses feature hills, valleys, and a variety of elevation changes. Due to the undulating landscape, golfers will frequently be faced with uneven lies. Hills and valleys challenge golfers with awkward stances and changes in ball flight. Knowing how to set up and what to expect will help you find your target in spite of sloping topography.

Uphill Lies

When your ball is on a slope that leads up to an elevated target, it's important to make a few adjustments.

1. Make sure your hips and shoulders are parallel with the slope (see photo). Resist the temptation to set up with your shoulders level with the horizon. This poor position will likely lead to the club hitting the ground too early, and at too steep an angle (a "fat" shot).

2. This uphill slope adds loft to your club—the ball will fly higher and shorter. The ball will also roll less when it lands. Be sure to "take more club" (a longer club) to make up for diminished distance.

3. Gravity makes it a little more difficult to turn through these shots aggressively. Weight tends to stay on the back foot and the clubface "closes"; therefore, these uphill shots will frequently fly a little left of your intended target line. On big slopes, be sure to aim just a touch right to compensate.

4. "Swing with the slope" is a great saying to remember: it will remind you not to chop steeply into the ground.

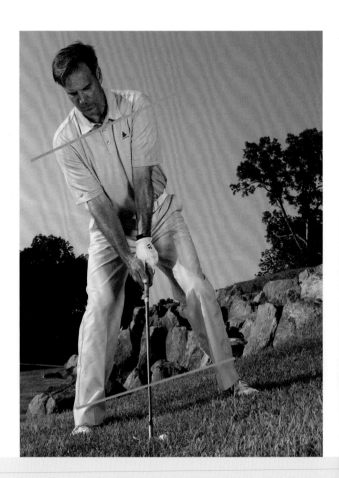

Downhill Lies

1. Make sure your hips and shoulders are parallel with the slope. If your shoulders are level with the horizon, you're likely to hit the ground before the ball, or "top" the ball (make contact above the ball's equator).

2. The downhill slope will take loft away from your club, effectively making it stronger than it would be from a level lie. Additionally, the ball will likely roll farther than normal after it lands. Be sure to "take less club" (a shorter club) to account for the greater distance.

3. Downhill shots tend to fly a bit to the right of your intended target line, so be sure to aim just a touch left.

4. Swing with the slope—the saying certainly works here as well. Trying to lift the ball or swinging up too fast will result in poor contact.

Take a Swing—Or Two!

When a golf ball is significantly above your feet or below your feet, your swing will be affected. In these awkward circumstances, it is important to take a few rehearsal swings and focus on finding your balance.
When faced with an uneven lie, take an extra practice swing or two to get comfortable and find solid footing.

Sidehill Lies (Above)

1. The higher a ball is above your feet, the flatter or more horizontal your swing becomes. It actually starts to feel more like a baseball swing. A ball that's above your feet will tend to fly to the left, and even continue to curve to the left. Make sure you aim a bit to the right of your intended target to account for this flight.

2. A ball that "draws" or curves to the left for a right-handed player will usually roll farther than normal after it lands. You may want to choose a shorter club (one with more loft) to adjust for the greater distance.

3. When the ball is above your feet, you're actually closer to the ball. To make up for this, "choke down" on the club so that you don't hit the ground too early.

Sidehill Lies (Below)

1. With the ball below your feet, the club will naturally sit with the toe a bit lower than the heel. This position will often launch the ball to the right of your intended target line, and the ball is likely to continue curving to the right. Be sure to aim a bit left of your target to prepare for a left-to-right flight.

2. A ball that flies left to right usually gets shorter distance and tends to roll less after landing. Choose a longer, less lofted club (for example, take an 8-iron instead of a 9-iron) to make up for the loss of distance.

3. Widen your stance a touch and grip the very end of the club. Those adjustments will help you reach the ball comfortably when it's below you.

With all uneven lies, I strongly recommend a practice swing or two. It's important to find your balance and see where the club brushes the turf during these slightly awkward swings. After getting comfortable and finding your balance, step in, address the ball, and swing with confidence.

escaping the woods

Even the best players find themselves in the woods once in a while. The important thing is to stay calm, and remember that a smooth, clean strike is more important than distance. Although some tree situations feel rather dire, you usually have a number of options to consider. Take, for instance, the tree situation shown here. You have three options: if you have a great lie, and tons of confidence, you might choose a more aggressive escape route (window A). If the lie is a little worse, or you want to be safer, window B makes more sense. And sometimes, especially if you have a bad lie or have trouble envisioning success with option A or B, it's prudent to bite the bullet and pitch out to safety on the safest route possible (window C), even though it might not get you closer to the hole.

There will be times when trees limit the length of your backswing or your finish. It's usually helpful to take a club with the appropriate loft (that will avoid launching the ball into other trees or limbs), choke down, take a shorter backswing, and focus on clean contact. Remember that the main objective is to get out and to a spot that will allow the next swing to be comfortable. This is the time to play smart and get yourself back into position for your next shot. If you get too greedy, you're likely to spend even more time looking for your ball in the forest.

playing in the rain

While most enjoy golf when Mother Nature cooperates, the game can certainly be played in less favorable conditions. But you *must* learn the limitations. If there is lightning or any hint of an electrical storm, I insist you seek safe shelter immediately. Electricity is nothing to underestimate when you're carrying a bag of metal "lightning rods" down the fairway. A simple light rain, however, can be managed.

Step 1: Get the Right Equipment

It's very helpful to dress for the occasion. Water-resistant outerwear (rain pants, jacket, and bucket hat) can keep you relatively comfortable. You should also have a golf umbrella, waterproof golf shoes, and a few extra towels. The rain will soak through your golf glove, making the leather rather slippery. Since a slick glove makes it impossible to hold your club consistently, experienced players have several extra golf gloves safely stored in a plastic ziplock bag. Rain gloves are made from a special material that allows you to keep a firm grip on your clubs, even in the wettest conditions. I would recommend buying a pair if you know bad weather is likely.

Step 2: Prepare for the Change in Conditions

The rain will make thick rough even heavier and more difficult to swing through. If you miss the fairway, you'll find a greater challenge escaping the tall grass. Be prepared to choose a safer play. Instead of trying to muscle the ball all the way to the green, pick a club with plenty of loft, and focus on advancing the ball into better position in the fairway. You'll notice that the ball doesn't roll much after landing on wet turf. Choose a club that will fly the ball a little farther in the air, because the ball is likely to stop right where it lands. Also, wet greens become significantly slower than greens in optimal conditions. Be sure to give your putts a little extra speed so they can reach the hole!

Step 3: Adjust, but Stick to Your Routine

Many players get frustrated in poor conditions. Fumbling with towels, umbrellas, and rain gear can get annoying. There will be a temptation to speed up your tempo, abandon practice swings, and possibly lose your patience. Remember that everyone on the golf course is dealing with the same challenges; the players who stay calm and focused will shoot better scores. Take a deep breath and settle into a rhythm. Take the extra time to dry off your grips, and find a place to leave your umbrella and towel. But continue to visualize your shots, take practice swings, and read putts as you would under normal conditions. Golf rewards those who stay calm and manage themselves best during difficult conditions.

playing in the wind

Wind can be even more challenging than rain in some circumstances. A strong wind can certainly influence the flight of your ball, so an adjustment may be required at address. Here's how you can adjust your swing for strong wind:

- If the wind is blowing strongly from left to right, set up aiming left of where you want the ball to land. Take your normal swing and allow the wind to push your ball back toward the target.

- If the wind is blowing from right to left, you'll need to set up aiming to the right of your target, and allow the ball to drift left in the breeze.

- Wind from the side will not have a huge effect on distance, but it will slow the ball down a touch. In most cases, taking an extra club would be prudent.

- If the wind is at your back, or "helping," you should choose a shorter and more lofted club. If the helping wind is very strong, you might be surprised how far your ball will fly (for example, an 8-iron may fly the distance you normally hit a 6-iron), so be sure to adjust accordingly.

- The most challenging situation is when the wind is blowing directly at you from your target. Most golfers naturally try to swing too hard to fight the wind's power. When you overswing, you're likely to lose balance or mis-hit the ball, leading to very poor results. The trick to playing straight into the wind is to take a longer or less lofted club, and make a smooth, comfortable swing.

There's an old saying to remember: "When it's breezy, swing easy." It's far better to choose a stronger club and stay centered and balanced. Smooth tempo and clean contact will lead to the best results.

troubleshooting your swing

I've discussed equipment and the golf course, and described how to play a wide variety of shots. But golf shots don't always work out the way we want them to. Of course the more you play and practice, the better you'll get, but it's nice to know how to adjust your swing along the way.

There are so many sources of golf instruction and "helpful" tips: books, magazines, videos, television shows, infomercials—even other golfers you play with. I encourage you to enjoy them all, but be very cautious! The golf swing is a very personal thing. A tip from a golf magazine may work for you but have a negative effect on another player's swing. Even the best players in the world have motions that differ significantly from one another. So don't try too hard to swing exactly like someone else—there's always room for individual style. This book concentrates on basic fundamentals and the solid components of a stable, repeatable golf swing.

But what should you do when golf shots consistently fail to find the target?

In this chapter, we'll look at six of the most aggravating shot results and their likely causes, and discuss divot patterns and what you can learn from them. So if you're wondering what causes the ball to curve off to one side or the other, why you're hitting the ground first, or how your wrists should look at the top of the swing, all these questions and more will be answered here.

six frustrating golf shots

Although the touring golf professionals make it look easy on television, golf can certainly be challenging at times. The first step toward improvement is to understand the cause of a disappointing golf shot. Be patient and don't get frustrated!

Following are the six most annoying problems, what causes them, and how you can correct them.

The Whiff

Many don't consider the whiff to be a shot at all, since the whiff is a swing that doesn't make contact with the ball. But whenever there is intent to hit the ball, that swing counts as a stroke—even if you don't touch the ball. First of all, understand that missing the ball entirely is not uncommon when you first start learning the game.

Common Causes of the Whiff

Rising during the backswing. When a golfer "stands up" during the backswing and doesn't get back down to the height he had at address.

Using the arms too much. Golfers who swing hard with their arms often bend their left elbow too much during the downswing. The bent elbow equals a "shorter" arm, which means the club won't get down to the ball.

Swaying and swinging off the back foot. When a golfer "slides" his weight to the right foot during the backswing, then swings too hard with the upper body and remains on his right foot too long. The result? The swing bottom is too far behind and the club rises up over the ball.

How to Cure the Whiff

Try to maintain your height at address all the way through impact. Relax your arms and let them swing freely without tension—the left arm should be relatively "long" as you swing through the ball. Remember that you need to swing down through the ball (don't try to lift it!) and finish on your left side.

The Shank

The shank happens when the ball is accidentally struck by the hosel or neck of the clubhead. The typical result is a ball that launches low and severely to the right. The sound of the shot is different, and the feel and look of the shot are both unpleasant.

Common Causes of the Shank

Too close to the ball at address. It takes a while for beginning golfers to get comfortable with how far they need to be from the ball at address. If they set up too close to the ball, they are likely to contact the hosel of the club once in a while.

Moving forward during the backswing or downswing. If a golfer's head moves closer to the ball during the backswing or downswing, it is likely that the hosel could come in contact with the ball.

"Throwing" the hands. Some golfers throw their hands out (significantly further from their body) during the downswing. If your hands are closer to the ball, the hosel comes into play.

How to Cure the Shank

Stand a little taller and a touch farther from the ball at address, and make sure to stay centered as you turn back and through the ball. Imagine that you're not getting closer to the ball during the swing. Also, try to keep your right elbow closer to your body as you turn through the shot.

The Slice

The slice is the most common trajectory in golf. It happens when the clubface is open to (or pointing slightly to the right of) the path your club is swinging on. Most golfers who slice end up aiming way to the left, and allowing the ball to slice back to the right. The problem is that a slicer is always losing power. A slice is a glancing blow that cuts across the ball causing sidespin and a massive loss of distance.

Common Causes of the Slice

Weak grip position. A weak grip position, where the left hand is rotated too far counter-clockwise (and "under" the grip), is likely to open the clubface during the swing and cause a slice.

Ball position. Slicers often put the ball too far forward in their stance (too close to the target). This forward position leads to a swing path that moves too far to the left and across the ball, creating a slicing sidespin.

Fast shoulders. Many golfers turn their hips through the shot, they rush, and start the downswing with their shoulders and arms before the lower body has a chance to rotate. Fast shoulders lead to a swing that cuts across the ball to the left, creating sidespin that curves a ball to the right.

How to Cure the Slice

Rotate your grip clockwise on the club into a slightly stronger position. Bring the ball back a bit toward the center of your stance and try not to rush the downswing with your shoulders. This will allow the clubface to square up while the club swings more to the right of your target line which will straighten out your shots!

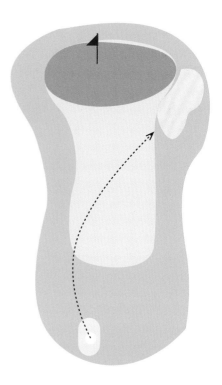

The Hook

Basically the opposite of the slice, a hooked shot is the result of the clubface being closed to (or facing to the left of) the path your club is swinging on. A hook usually starts a bit right of the target line then curves sharply to the left. Most golfers who hook the ball aim way to the right and allow the hook to bring the ball back toward the target. Hooked shots generally stay low and curve to the ground too quickly, but they tend to roll along the ground for quite a distance.

Common Causes of the Hook

Alignment. Most golfers who hook the ball have a stance that is too closed, meaning a line drawn across their toes would point to the right of their target line. This setup leads to a swing that comes to the ball dramatically from the "inside" (from close to the body then out across the ball), creating hook spin.

Strong grip position. If the hands are rotated too far clockwise (right hand is too far under the grip), the hands are likely to "close" the club (turn the clubface to the left) during the swing, creating hook spin.

Swing plane is too shallow. This means that the club is swinging too horizontally around the body, which tends to curve the ball from right to left.

How to Cure the Hook

Make sure an imaginary line across your toes is parallel to your target line. "Weaken" your grip a bit by rotating it counterclockwise a little. Then try to swing the club "up" and lift your hands a touch higher during the backswing.

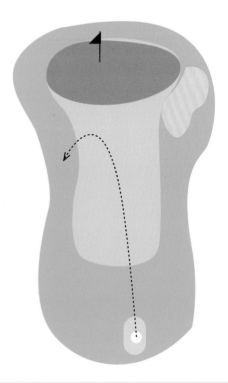

The Fat Shot

The fat shot takes place when you accidentally hit the ground before the ball. In golf it's critical to strike the ball with a descending blow, hitting the "little ball" (golf ball) before the "big ball" (planet Earth). With the fat shot, your club will enter the ground too early and turf will be trapped between the clubface and the ball. That takes all the speed away from the shot, and your ball will only fly a very short distance. Additionally, the fat shot can deliver a lot of shock to your hands, wrists, and arms.

Common Causes of the Fat Shot

Lowering during the swing. Some golfers, especially those who try too hard, will get lower to the ground during the downswing in an effort to ensure contact with the ball. This can lead to "digging" or fat shots.

Not enough body turn. If a golfer swings the club up and down without much body rotation, the club tends to swing too vertically or "steeply." The result is a very sharp descent that tends to get caught in the turf before making contact with the ball.

Ball position. If the ball is too far back in the stance (too close to the right foot), the golfer will need to swing the club downward abruptly during the swing. The quick change of direction and the sharp descent required to hit the ball can lead to fat shots.

How to Cure the Fat Shot

Make sure you maintain your height at address all the way through impact; be careful not to increase your spine angle or your knee flex. Also make sure the ball is positioned a touch farther forward in your stance and remember to make a graceful body turn.

The Thin Shot

A thin shot occurs when the leading edge of your club strikes the ball near or just below its equator. A thin shot stays relatively low, and can take off like a bullet and travel much farther than desired. If your club strikes the ball above the equator, the ball won't even get off the ground. This *very* thin contact is called "topping" the ball. The thin or topped shot is a close cousin of the whiff, just not quite as dramatic.

Common Causes of the Thin Shot

Ball position. If the ball is too far forward, a golfer may catch it thin as the club rises up to the finish. If the ball is severely back in the stance, the club may strike it too early on the way down from the top of the backswing. For other likely causes, look back to the whiff.

How to Cure the Thin Shot

As with the whiff, it's important to maintain your height from address through impact. Let your arms relax so you swing easily and without tension. Keep your left arm long, and swing down through the ball rather than try to lift it.

Topping the ball

Hitting just below the equator

Wrist Position at the Top of Your Backswing

There are many ways to get the job done in golf, and styles vary significantly from one player to the next. But certain positions lead to certain tendencies. That's definitely the case with wrist positions at the top of your swing. Where your wrist is positioned can have a significant impact on the shape or curve of your ball flight. It might be helpful to check your position in a mirror from time to time to make sure it's consistently in the position that leads to the best results. Following are the three possible wrist positions at the top of a swing.

Cupped: This position is common in players with more upright or vertical swings. For many golfers, the cupped wrist can lead to swings that are too steep. This position will also tend to leave the clubface open a bit, leading to shots that launch to the right and/or slice. Two examples of golfers who play very well with a cupped wrist are John Daly and Fred Couples.

Bowed: This position is common in players with "flatter" or more horizontal swings. For many players, the bowed wrist can lead to a lower ball flight that tends to go to the left or hook. Graeme MacDowell and Dustin Johnson are two golfers who play well with a bowed wrist position.

Square: This is the position I recommend. Although success can certainly be found with the other two, this square position will generally lead to the most consistent results. Note that the clubface at the top is parallel with the back of the left wrist and left forearm. Golfers who have succeeded with this flat position include Tiger Woods and Justin Rose.

playing the game

arriving at the golf course

When you plan to meet a friend and play tennis at the park, the entire scenario seems fairly straightforward. You put on a pair of shorts, lace up your sneakers, grab a racquet and some tennis balls, and head to the courts. Going to play golf at a course for the first time can be a bit more confusing. Although there are many kinds of golf facilities, and each one is somewhat different from the next, I'll walk you through the typical arrival procedure. I'll identify and discuss several key people, places, and things you're likely to see before stepping onto the first tee. Knowing what you're likely to find, who you're likely to meet, and the appropriate actions to take will ease your mind and help to make the day a more enjoyable experience.

After checking in and warming up, we'll head to the course. I'll walk you through the entire process and point out a number of signs, items, and structures you may see during and after your round. Of course, each facility is different, but knowing what you're likely to find and what it's there for will help you feel comfortable and make the most out of your visit.

before you go to the course

Call Ahead

Since your friend invited you, it's possible that he or she will pay for your greens fees—but not necessarily! You should know what all associated costs for the day will be, so that you can be prepared. Find out the greens fees (the amount charged for you to play 18 holes), the golf cart fee (some courses require cart usage), and fore-caddie fees. Even if you ride, some courses send a fore-caddie out with each group to assist with care of the course and to help find golf balls, etc. If you and your host prefer to walk and take a caddie, you should ask what the caddie rates are. Many public and resort courses don't have caddies, but may have pull carts available as an alternative to carrying your own bag.

Other questions you should ask while on the call: Assuming you don't have your own equipment, ask if they rent clubs and how much it will cost. You should also find out if they have a practice range where you can warm up prior to the round. Another question would be regarding dress code (see the following), and what restrictions they may have. The bottom line? Make a call or check the club website and find out as much as you can *before* arriving at the club. You want to be as prepared as possible!

Know the (Dress) Code

Although dress restrictions at golf courses have relaxed in recent years, you should still try to dress the part—and it's always best to err on the formal side! To be safe: stay away from any denim, cut-off shorts, cargo shorts (with big pockets on the outer thigh), t-shirts, tank tops, sandals, and any shoes with sharp or high heels. Just wear a pair of casual non-denim slacks and a collared golf shirt (tucked in) and you'll be fine. At some courses golf shoes are required (and are seldom available to rent), so you might want to purchase a pair ahead of time. Other courses are fine with flat soled sneakers or boat shoes. *Do not borrow* an old pair of golf shoes that have metal spikes in them. Metal spikes are not allowed on most golf courses, and clacking down the sidewalk in them is a sure way to tell everyone "I'm not a golfer!"

what to expect upon arrival

So let's assume a friend of yours knows you're looking to play golf and invites you to his club. He tells you that he has reserved a 9:00 A.M. tee time. The first thing you want to do is communicate to your friend that this is your first time to visit a golf course. He will certainly want to ease your mind and answer any questions you have, but in case you don't have a chance to touch base before arriving at the course, I am happy to be your golf facility tour guide! I would also add that it's always a good idea to arrive early, to give yourself plenty of time to get comfortable at the club before your tee-time (it's important to arrive at the first tee five minutes *before* your tee-time).

Bag Drop

When you first drive in to a golf club, you may see a sign that says "Bag Drop." If you have your own equipment, you should stop your car, pop the trunk, take out your clubs, and set them down on the rack. There may be a staff member to greet you and confirm your name and starting time, and ask whom you might be playing with. After dropping off your bag, park your car and change your shoes. If the facility has a locker room, don't change your shoes in the parking lot; bring them with you to the clubhouse.

Pro Shop

In most cases, the first place you'll head after parking the car is to the pro shop. The pro shop is often located within the main clubhouse, and this is where you'll check in and pay for greens fees, cart fees, and any other supplies you may need (rental clubs, golf balls, glove, cap, tees, etc.). You might also ask about the practice range availability—the counter attendant might be able to sell you a bucket of balls for the driving range at this point.

Locker Room

The next stop is usually the locker room. This is where you will likely find an attendant who will assign you a locker. If you plan on changing clothes before or after your round, the locker is a very helpful option. You may also want to bring some rain gear (jacket, pants, hat, gloves, umbrella, towels), and if you don't leave them in your car, don't have room in your bag, and don't need them immediately, the locker is the place to store them. The locker room will sometimes offer sunblock, which you should take advantage of. After changing into your golf shoes, leave your other shoes in front of the locker if you'd like them shined; if not, put them inside the locker. If you return from your round and the shoes you left have been polished nicely, you should tip the attendant (appropriate amounts vary, so check with your host).

Caddie Master/Outside Operations

Once you leave the locker room and head outside, the first stop is usually a structure near the first tee. Here you will find a caddie master or starter who will set you up with the clubs you rented, show you to your cart, direct you to the practice range, and clarify your starting time. He will also assign you a caddie if that is an option you've chosen. If you're at a club that uses caddies, the caddie master would be the person to ask about rates and appropriate amounts to tip (if you have a caddie who does a nice job and helps you enjoy your round).

Driving Range

It's always a good plan to leave enough time to warm up on the practice range. The important thing is to loosen up at a smooth pace. Don't feel the need to hit a thousand balls; just warm up with an easy tempo. Some driving ranges indicate yardages so that you can dial in your distances with each club. Relax, find your rhythm, and focus on a few good thoughts that you've picked up here in this book. (In fact, you may want to keep a copy in your golf bag!) Some ranges have limitations regarding what clubs you can hit, and where to hit from. Take extra care to read any signage on or near the range, and always be careful of other players, and where they're swinging—always err on the side of safety!

Practice Putting Green

Usually near the first tee you'll find a practice putting green. As with all putting greens, the only club you should use on this turf is a putter. Many clubs prohibit chipping and pitching shots to a practice putting green. Be sure to obey all signage, and ask the caddie master or starter if you're unsure. It's important to take at least a few putts on the practice green before going to the first tee. This green is maintained to the same specifications as the greens on the course, and you'll be able to practice your putting stroke and get a good feel for speed.

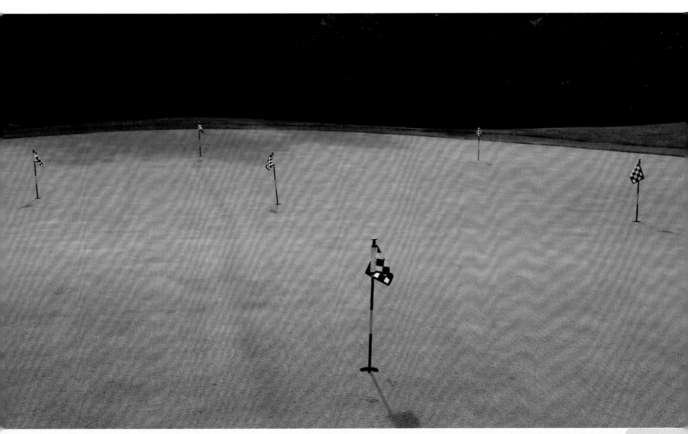

what you'll find on the course

You may come across some odd, unfamiliar objects along the course. Following are some of the most common and what they are for.

Tee Markers

The scorecard will indicate different total yardages from different sets of tees. Find the set that plays to an appropriate yardage for your current level of ability (the better and more experienced the player, the longer the course they can handle). For example, if you feel a course of 6,200 yards is good for you, and that length is associated with the "white" tees on the scorecard, then you will look for the white tee markers on the teeing ground of each hole, and play from there. Some courses have as many as five different tee marker settings to choose from.

Halfway House

It's called the "halfway house" because usually it's located somewhere near the halfway point of the round (between the 9th and 10th holes). This is usually where you can use the restroom, order and eat lunch, or just get a snack or a beverage to keep your energy up for the remainder of your 18 holes.

Yardage Plates

Yardage plates tell exactly how many yards in distance from the plate to the middle of the green on the particular hole you are playing. They are usually located in the ground on the tee box. Common yardage plates (also known as "yardage markers") are also located down the middle of most holes. The usual plate distances are 200 yards (183m) to the center of the green (usually blue, if colors are used), 150 yards (137m) (usually white), and 100 yards (91m) (usually red). Additionally, yardages to the center of the green are sometimes stamped into sprinkler heads that can be found randomly throughout the fairways. The important thing to remember is that the distance indicated is to the middle of the green on that hole.

Tee Sign

Many courses feature a tee sign near the teeing ground of each hole. These signs typically tell the golfer which hole this is, what par is for the hole and the distance to the hole from the different tee markers. Some signs also indicate the handicap of the hole, which is a number that tells how difficult that hole is (#18 hdcp is the easiest hole on the course, and #1 hdcp is the hardest hole on the course). Some signs even have an overhead view of the layout of the hole.

Ball Washers

Near the teeing ground of certain holes, you will find a ball washing machine. Course conditions will often get your golf ball a bit dirty. Use these machines to quickly clean your ball (but don't use the machine while another player is preparing to swing!). They come in different models, and some have brushes down near the base that can be used for cleaning the bottom of your golf shoes.

Lightning Shelter

As the name implies, these small structures are designed to provide safe shelter during an electrical storm. Not all golf courses have these shelters, but those that have them do offer a greater level of safety for golfers. The best course of action is to get back to the clubhouse, but if the lightning sneaks up on you quickly and you can't get back to home base, find and remain in one of these shelters until the storm passes. If the shelter is not specifically built to protect from lightning, there is no real benefit, so hopefully you can find your way back to the clubhouse before the storm gets too strong!

how the game is played

New golfers often spend much of their time practicing, going to the driving range, and taking lessons from PGA instructors. While I admire and encourage all of that, don't forget that *playing the game* is the ultimate goal! I've actually heard many beginners say, "I'm practicing and taking lessons; someday I'll be good enough to play." I understand that the beginner is hoping to find a level of competency before stepping onto the first tee, but most people wait too long before enjoying the on-course experience. Get out there and play! These days, PGA instructors who work at golf courses are trying to give more and more "playing lessons." This style of instruction takes new golfers out to the course and helps them understand the swing and how to use it in various real situations. The playing lesson is also a chance to show beginners how to conduct themselves in the golf course environment.

Yes, etiquette and the rules are both important in golf. But consider this chapter your own personal lesson on how to actually play the game. I'll take you through a round of golf step by step, and explain many of the subtleties and procedures that experienced players often take for granted.

before your round

Choosing Your Golf Partners

Playing the game starts with a choice: Who are you going to play with? Well, there are a number of possibilities. You could play alone as a single; you could round up one, two, or three friends who play golf and would love to join you; or you could call the course and say you would like to be paired with another player or group of players. If you do decide to call and ask to join another group, make sure the person taking the call knows you're a beginner. Ideally you'll be placed with golfers who are accommodating and encouraging, and perhaps relatively new to the game as well.

Arriving at the First Tee

Let's assume you're given a tee-time of 10:00 A.M., and you're going to join three other golfers you've never met before. Of the three, one is a beginner like you, and the other two have both played golf for a few years and know the rules and procedures well. After arriving at the course, checking in, and warming up, you should be near the first tee at 9:50 A.M. or earlier. It's important to arrive at the first tee with plenty of time to meet your fellow players and decide whether you'd like to play a match or just play your own ball against the course.

Choosing Sides for a Match

If you decide to play a match, you need to choose partners or create "sides" (teams). It's customary to try to make the sides evenly matched. In this case, one of the experienced players and one of the beginners would form a side against the other two. Teams can also be chosen randomly. This is sometimes done with a "ball toss." One player holds each of the four golf balls from the group in one hand. He then tosses the four balls up into the air. After all four land, the players who own the two balls that are closest together on the ground will be a team. It's also important for all four players to decide upon a format of play, agree on the appropriate rules, and make sure everyone agrees on the "action"—any modest wagers that might take place. Agreement upon all format and financial issues before the first shot is important, and will avoid any awkward moments during or after the round.

playing the game

Who Has the Honor?

The person, or in this case the team, who hits first has the "honor." On the first tee, the honor is chosen randomly. Teams could stand facing each other and flip a tee into the air. The team that the tee points to will go first. You could also determine the order of play by flipping a coin, drawing straws, picking a number out of a hat, or simply asking "Who's ready?" But as the match goes on to the second tee and beyond, the honor always goes to the "side" (team) who won the previous hole (or the side that had the better score). If the previous hole was tied (or "halved"), the order will remain the same as it was on the tee of that previous hole.

During the play of a hole, the player who is farthest from the cup always goes first—unless all players agree to play "ready golf." Rather than always waiting for the proper order of play, ready golf is a casual format that encourages players to play when ready. This style of play is popular when you feel your group is playing slowly and you need to pick up the pace of play. You still need to be respectful of other golfers in the group and play safely, but ready golf can help to move things along.

Getting Ready for Your Turn

A few tips before you start your round:

1. Mark your ball with a felt-tip marker. Make a distinguishing mark on the ball so that you don't confuse your ball with someone else's.

2. Have an extra ball in your pocket. If you hit your first ball out of bounds, you want to be ready to hit another ball. Running back to the cart and rummaging through your bag to find another ball is cumbersome and takes extra time. Most golfers will allow you to hit a second (provisional) ball right after hitting your first, but you may want to wait until the rest of your group has teed off before taking a second swing.

3. Most golfers take a practice swing or two before addressing the ball for the actual shot. Don't take too many practice swings (the limit should be two), and make sure you keep the practice swings "above ground." Taking divots with practice swings is a no-no. And try not to take too much time with your pre-shot routine.

4. Be prepared! You should know which club you want to use *before* it's your turn to play. You should find out the yardage, grab a few clubs (always take one stronger and one weaker than the club you think you'll need in case the wind kicks up, or in case you simply change your mind), and position yourself near your ball. When it's your turn, you'll be ready for action!

"Fore!"

If you happen to accidentally hit a shot that's heading toward other golfers, it's imperative that you yell "Fore!" to warn them of your wayward shot. And you should yell loud enough for them to hear you clearly!

What Is a "Mulligan"?

After hitting your first tee shot into the woods on the right, the two players on the opposing team say, "Take a mulligan." A mulligan is a do-over. It's not uncommon for players to take or offer a mulligan (sometimes referred to as a "breakfast ball") on the first tee. Although not allowed in the Rules of Golf, mulligans on the first tee have become accepted at certain clubs and by many players. They are never to take place in an official tournament, but if you're playing a casual round and the group you're playing with wants to allow it, why not?

Incidentally, if your second ball also flies into the woods, I would recommend *not* hitting a third ball. With penalty strokes, hitting the third ball is actually taking your 5th stroke—and chances are you won't be helping your partner much at this point. It would usually be better to say, "I'll take a quick look for those two … if I can't find one of them, I'll just pick up on this hole and drop another ball up by you guys for practice. Partner, this hole is all you." Most groups will appreciate your willingness to move the game along.

Players at Different Teeing Grounds

If you choose to play from the white tees, you will tee up from the white tee on each hole you play during your round of golf. You should tee up your ball within the rectangle formed by the two tee markers, and an imaginary point located two club-lengths behind each marker.

If a player in your group is playing from a more forward set of tees, that player should really go last in the tee shot rotation regardless of score. Even if they shot the low score on the previous hole and have the honor, it would be awkward and time-consuming to have them walk up to the forward tee, hit their shot, and walk back to the tee everyone else is playing from to wait while the others hit. The player should allow those farthest from the green to tee off first, then walk forward with the group and tee off at the forward tees. This routine is widely accepted and is very efficient.

Pace of Play

Keeping pace with the group ahead of you is one of the most important rules in golf. Always be wary of slow play! Being prepared when it's your turn to play can help. It's also a good idea to write down scores *after* you've left the putting surface. Nobody wants to wait in the fairway behind you while you tabulate all the scores for your group. Move off the putting green after holing out, and do any scoring once you return to your cart or make your way to the next teeing ground.

If for some reason you or your group is exceptionally slow and there are groups waiting behind you, you should move off to the side and wave the faster players through. Then try your best to pick up the pace a bit and keep up with them.

The Tap-In

Speaking of pace of play, slow putting procedures on the green are usually the biggest culprit. Be sure to mark your ball, fix your ball mark, and "read" the green *prior* to your turn. When it's your turn to putt, just replace your ball, remove the ball mark, take a practice stroke or two, and take a roll at it. If you miss the cup by just a few inches, it's okay to ask your opponents, "Mind if I finish?" They will certainly say to go ahead, and even though your ball is closer to the hole than theirs, you're welcome to "tap in" quickly and get out of the way. This keeps the pace of play moving nicely. If you aren't sure whether you can make the putt, you're always entitled to mark the position of your ball and step away to await your next turn.

Halfway House Etiquette

Many golfers like to stop in the middle of their round to grab a quick lunch at the halfway house where food and beverages are available. If your group stops to rest or have a bite and the group behind you doesn't want to stop, you should let them pass and go to the next tee in front of you.

Scoring

Once you've completed 9 holes, the scores are typically tallied and announced. These scores represent totals for what is known as the "front nine." At this point participants will get a good feeling of where the match stands, and they may even modify the wager. Holes 10 through 18 are considered the "back nine" and should also be totaled. Then the front and back nine scores are added together for the total score.

Post-Round

Once the match is complete, you should shake hands with your partner and the members of the opposing team and all caddies. I also strongly recommend settling any wagers immediately! Your group might want to settle your bets and toast the highlights of the match over a round of drinks. Spending some time at the "19th hole" (the bar or lounge) is customary, and one of the fun social aspects of golf. Enjoy it!

the basic rules

I'll be honest: the rules of golf are fairly intricate. The official rule book is filled with text that outlines every possible scenario, and provides a detailed procedure for each one of them. Although the book is well written and very thorough, the rules of the game can be overwhelming and rather intimidating—especially for a beginner. But *fear not!* In this chapter, I have chosen 12 key rules of the game, and described them in basic terms. It's important to note that the most important "rules" of golf are respecting the course, your equipment, and other golfers, and playing at an appropriate pace.

Unless you're posting official scores, entered in a tournament, or playing a match with other golfers in your group, there's no need to get too concerned about each and every rule. Have fun … there will be plenty of time to learn the necessary rules as you become more involved with this sport. Ultimately, I strongly encourage you to read through the official rule book for more details and specifics, but in the meantime this chapter can serve as a simple guide. Follow these rules and you'll feel comfortable with your actions on the golf course.

Rule #1: Clubs

You are only allowed to possess a maximum of 14 clubs when you play golf (13 clubs plus a putter). The most common error happens when a player is "trying out a new club" and forgets to take out the club it is supposed to replace. All 14 clubs must also conform with USGA specifications (most on the market do conform), and cannot be bent or damaged significantly.

Rule #2: Teeing Ground

Once you decide which tee markers to play from, you need to tee up the ball properly. The ball can be placed on a tee only for the first shot of every hole (and note that using a tee for your ball is not mandatory, but generally preferred). Make sure the ball is teed up within the imaginary rectangle formed by the two tee markers and two imaginary points that are two club-lengths behind the markers. Keep in mind that you are permitted to stand outside this imaginary zone, but the ball *must* be within that rectangle.

Rule #3: Order of Play

Who plays first? The order of play can be totally random on the first tee, but after those first shots of the round, the order will be defined. The person whose ball lies the farthest from the cup will always play first. On the next tee, it's the player with the best score on the previous hole who will get the honor of hitting first. Next to tee off will be the player with the second best score, and so on. If two players have the same score, the order from the previous tee will decide who goes first.

Rule #4: A Lost Ball

If you hit a poor shot and fear that the ball might be lost, you should take another ball. Announce that you are hitting a "provisional," drop it as near as possible and no closer to the hole than the last shot you took (or re-tee the ball if it was a shot from a teeing ground), and hit this second ball. You will have no more than five minutes to look for the first ball. If you can't find it within that time, the provisional ball becomes the ball you are playing (just add two penalty strokes to your score for that hole).

Rule #5: Play It as It Lies

"Play it as it lies" is one of the easiest rules to remember. It's one of the most important rules of the game. There are certain circumstances where you are entitled to mark, lift, and drop your ball in a different area (I will address some of them later in this list), but for the most part, you should not touch your ball unless you are on the teeing ground (before playing your tee shot) or on the green (after you've marked the position of your ball). Many golfers are tempted to improve the position of their ball during the play of a hole. They might want to "fluff" it up a little bit when it's lying in the rough, or move it into a nicer position in the fairway, but those actions are not allowed. Regardless of how bad the lie is, you are expected to play the shot without touching the ball or moving it prior to your swing.

Rule #6: A Stroke

A stroke is the forward movement of your club with the intent to hit the ball. Each stroke counts toward your score. Practice swings are not strokes. If you accidentally knock your ball off the tee, it's not a stroke. But if you swing at the ball and intend to hit it, it counts as a stroke. If you swing and whiff, or miss the ball entirely, it counts as a stroke. You may be the only one who knows whether you actually intended to hit the ball. Always be honest!

Rule #7: Out of Bounds

Out of bounds (also known as "O.B.") is usually defined by white stakes. If you hit a ball beyond the O.B. stakes, you are not allowed to play that ball. You must replay the shot with another ball and add two strokes to the score you make on that hole with the second ball.

Rule #8: "Unplayable"

If your ball is in a horrible spot, you may declare the ball "unplayable." The player is the sole judge of whether a ball is truly unplayable. You now have three options: 1. Drop the ball correctly (outstretched arm at shoulder height) within two club-lengths but no closer to the hole. 2. Go back to the point of your last shot, and drop as near as possible to that point but no nearer the hole. 3. Draw an imaginary line from the cup back through the point where your ball lies. You can drop anywhere behind the ball away from the hole and on that line. In all cases, you will add one penalty stroke to your score for the hole.

Rule #9: Obstructions and Loose Impediments

Loose impediments are natural objects like stones, twigs, leaves, pine cones, etc. These objects can be moved (carefully, without moving your ball) out of the way of your swing or shot without penalty, provided they are not firmly fixed or growing and you are not in a hazard. Obstructions are artificial objects or surfaces that cannot be moved (cart paths, drainage covers, water fountains, etc.). You are permitted to take a free drop within one club-length of the nearest point of relief, without a penalty. Moveable obstructions are artificial objects that you are permitted to move without penalty, such as chairs, water coolers, cart signs, etc.

Rule #10: Bunkers

When you are in a sand bunker, it's important to know that you cannot touch the sand prior to your downswing. You cannot rest the clubhead on the sand, or touch sand during the takeaway/backswing. To avoid a penalty, you must "hover" the club above the sand at address, complete your backswing, then splash through the sand on your way to the finish.

Rule #11: Water Hazards

If you hit your ball into a water hazard (marked with yellow lines or stakes), you have three options: 1. Play the ball as it lies, from within the hazard lines. 2. Replay the last shot and add two strokes to your score with the second ball. 3. Draw an imaginary line back from the cup through the point where your ball last crossed the hazard line. You can drop anywhere on that line, and add a penalty stroke. With lateral water hazards (water marked with red lines or stakes), you have the first three options plus two more: 1. Find the point where the ball last crossed the hazard, and drop a ball within two club-lengths but no closer to the hole, and add one stroke. 2. You could also go to a spot that's the same distance from the hole on the other side of the hazard, take a drop, and add a stroke.

Rule #12: The Flag

If you are just off the putting surface, you may chip or putt your ball toward the cup without removing the flag. In fact, some golfers feel that the flag will act as a backstop and help to deflect the ball into the hole. But if your ball is on the green, the flagstick must be removed before the ball makes it to the hole. A caddie or even a fellow golfer can "tend" the flag, or hold the flag while keeping the bottom of it in the cup (so that you can see where the hole is from long range). But they must remove it before the ball reaches the cup. If a ball on the green rolls into the flagstick, the player is assessed a two-stroke penalty.

keeping score

One of my favorite quotes regarding golf scoring comes from the best golf movie ever made, *Caddyshack:*

> *Judge Smails (Ted Knight): Ty, what did you shoot today?*
> *Ty Webb (Chevy Chase): Oh, Judge, I don't keep score.*
> *Judge Smails: Then how do you measure yourself with other golfers?*
> *Ty Webb: By height.*

Okay, maybe you don't share my sense of humor, but trust me, *Caddyshack* is a classic. It is also, by far, the most quoted golf movie. You will hear references to this movie throughout your golf career. I strongly encourage new golfers to watch the film—you'll be glad you did! (Warning: it's rated R.)

When you first begin to learn golf, the emphasis should not be on scoring. But as you grow comfortable with the sport and begin to improve and play with other golfers, keeping score properly becomes important. Keeping score not only measures you against other golfers, it measures your performance against the golf course, and it provides a true indication of your progress. To a beginning golfer, the scoring process can be a bit intimidating. There are a number of scoring-related terms that may be unfamiliar, and even the process of proper score keeping can seem confusing. In this chapter, I will review the terms and definitions and explain the score-keeping process.

anatomy of a scorecard

Scorecards come in a variety of layouts, and every course has their own special version. Although there are some slight differences, there is basic information that most scorecards will have. Let's look at this sample card.

2 HOLE   **4** BLUE   **5** STROKES   **0**   Brian **1**   **3** PAR   **6**

HOLE	BLACK	BLUE	GOLD	STROKES	Brian			PAR			WHITE	GREEN
1	538	513	513	7				5			491	469
2	389	378	378	15				4			356	340
3	177	159	144	17				3			144	126
4	435	418	393	1				4			393	367
5	500	486	486	9				5			471	417
6	932	375	375	13				4			341	315
7	217	206	206	11				3			173	161
8	528	512	482	3				5			482	464
9	440	410	347	5				4			347	276
OUT	3616	3457	3324					37			3198	2935
10	390	362	362	12				4			337	314
11	197	175	158	16				3			158	125
12	601	579	553	2				5			553	526
13	417	375	354	8				4			354	318
14	157	138	138	18				3			121	89
15	521	502	502	4				5			485	444
16	359	337	337	10				4			307	289
17	247	191	170	14				3			170	150
18	414	394	356	6				4			356	325
IN	3303	3053	2930					35			2841	2580
TOT	6919	6510	6254					72			6039	5515
HANDICAP												
NET SCORE												

7 OUT   **8** IN   **9** HANDICAP

DATE   SCORER **10**   ATTEST **11**

1. Player's information. The name goes in the larger box, their handicap (if they have one) goes in the smaller box on top

2. The 18 holes.

3. The par score for the hole—the score expected from an accomplished player.

4. Yardage for the hole. That yardage will differ depending upon which set of tees you play from.

5. Strokes columns. These numbers indicate the difficulty of the holes—number 1 is the hardest, number 18 is the easiest.

6. Here is where you record how many strokes you took on each hole.

7. OUT (as in heading out, away from the clubhouse) is where you total your score for the first nine holes (or "front nine").

8. IN (as in coming in, or returning to the clubhouse) is where you total your score for the last nine holes (or "back nine").

9. In this sample, there is a space to indicate each player's course handicap, and a space for the net scores (actual or "gross" score minus course handicap).

10. This is where the scorekeeper's signature and the date go.

11. The attest is for the signature of another member of the group who is "attesting," or verifying the scores.

The different sets of tees are frequently described with colors. On this sample card, we have used the following colors:

Black tees are often the most challenging. They consist of longer yardages and should be played by professionals and very accomplished golfers.

Blue tees are often the next longest set of tees you could play from. They should also be played by better golfers who have low handicaps and can hit the ball with plenty of distance.

Gold tees offer a slightly shorter course that is suitable for an average player.

The **white** and **green** sets of tees are for shorter hitters and beginning golfers. These tees will provide a more playable and enjoyable length for novice players.

Many scorecards will also give you the course and slope ratings from different sets of tees for both men and women. These numbers indicate the difficulty level of the course you played and are very important if you plan on posting or submitting your card for handicap purposes.

understanding the process

In a tournament, official scorecards are normally handed out to each participant along with a rules sheet explaining the format of the event. In these cases, most of the scorecard work has been done for you. But I will help you go through the process on your own for a typical round of golf with a few friends or fellow golfers.

1. **Get a scorecard.** Scorecards are usually found on the steering wheel of the golf cart, so each member of the foursome has easy access to the card. In some cases, the pro shop attendant or starter (attendant at the first tee) will hand you a card or you can take one from a designated spot near the first tee.

2. **Choose your tees.** Look at the card and determine which set of tees you want to play from. There will be yardage totals at the bottom or far end of the card; the longer yardages are for more experienced players. If you're a beginner, you should try to stay with the shorter yardages.

3. **Choose a scorekeeper.** Write your name in the space provided, and if you offer to keep score for your entire group, write their names in as well. It's important to note that each player is responsible for knowing know how many strokes they have taken and for keeping their own score honestly and accurately. In fact, even if there is a designated "scorekeeper," you should keep track of your own scores on a separate scorecard (and you may want to keep the card so you can post your score in a handicap computer later).

4. **Note handicaps.** You may be scoring a match that involves handicaps. If so, you should put the player's course handicap next to their name. When scoring, your main objective is to put the number of strokes taken on each hole in the appropriate space on the card. Always put down the *gross* score. The *net* score (the gross score minus any handicap strokes that might be allotted on a given hole) can be figured out later, or on a separate line if desired.

5. **Total scores.**

6. **Check final scores.** In an official event, the scorekeeper will sign the card in the space provided, and another player who agrees with all the figures will "attest" the card by signing it as well.

Never stand on the putting surface and tabulate scores for everyone—that would slow down play and cause the group behind you to get rather angry. Instead, always "do the math" after returning to the carts, or figure out scores on the next tee so as not to hold up other players on the course. If keeping score for others in your foursome, always ask them politely for their score on the last hole.

common golf scoring terms

Par: The score a highly skilled golfer can be expected to make on that hole. For example, a par 4 should be completed in four strokes by an accomplished player.

Birdie: A score that is one stroke better or lower than the assigned par score for a hole. For example, if you needed only 4 strokes to complete a par-5 hole, you scored a birdie.

Eagle: A score that is two strokes better than par on a given hole.

Double Eagle: Yes, every once in a while, a great (or very lucky) player will hit their second shot into the hole on a par 5! A double eagle is a score that is three strokes better than par on a given hole.

Bogey: A score that is one stroke more or higher than the assigned par for a hole. If you require 4 strokes to get your ball in the hole on a par 3, you score a bogey.

Double Bogey: A score that is two strokes above par on a given hole.

Triple Bogey: A score that is three strokes above par on a given hole.

Quadruple Bogey: A "quad" is a score that is four strokes above or more than par on a given hole.

Snowman: A snowman is an eight (referring to the actual shape of the number itself), which would be a triple bogey on a par 5, or a "quad" on a par 4.

Ace: I hope you all get to record an "ace" at some point. An ace is another term for a "hole in one"—which means your tee shot goes in the hole on a par 3!

safety and etiquette

Golf is a sport that can be enjoyed by everyone. And like all sports, golf has rules and regulations that govern play and keep games and competitions fair. But golf is normally played without the watchful eye of an umpire or a referee. Golfers generally govern themselves, and even call penalties on themselves. In addition to knowing the rules, it's also the player's responsibility to observe proper etiquette and take necessary safety precautions. In this chapter, I'll introduce some very important points that will help you play golf safely, and with proper consideration for the golf course and other players. Playing with proper etiquette and consideration will benefit the conditions of the course and will also show respect to others.

safety

Thankfully, you won't need to fear being tackled by a 250-pound linebacker while you're lining up a putt, but disregard for safety can be very dangerous in golf. There are four key zones for golf safety: swinging the club, flight of the ball, the golf cart, and weather. Here's what you need to know to be safe on the course.

Swinging the Club

Golf safety starts long before you get to the first tee. Many golf club-related accidents take place on the range or while warming up, and trust me, getting struck with a club is incredibly painful and can cause serious harm. In golf, a player swings a chunk of heavy metal on a long metal shaft around his or her body. The club swings back behind the player, then back to the ball and on through to the finish, at very high speeds. A significant section of this sweeping arc is "blind"; it happens beyond the view of the person swinging the club.

The driving range is a place where many golfers are lined up to take swings toward a shared target. It's important that you always check behind you before swinging a club. Serious injuries can take place when a player grabs a club and takes a practice swing without realizing that another person, child, pet, or structure is within the "swing zone." As the person swinging, be sure to also take a look up; make sure you're clear of any light fixtures, fans, low ceilings, and so on.

You should also be wary of others who may swing without making sure the coast is clear. Don't expect the other guy to do the right thing and check the surroundings before swinging. Be sure to give yourself a wide cushion of space, both when you set up to take swings and as you walk past others. The same caution needs to take place while actually playing the game, especially when taking practice swings while you wait for your turn at the tee or when taking swings prior to your turn on the course.

Flight of the Ball

Getting struck by a golf club can cause serious pain—and getting hit by a golf ball is no picnic, either. *Never* strike a golf ball when there are other people in front of you and within range. Even if you're pretty sure you can't reach people who are in front of you, *don't hit!* Wait until there is no chance of hitting them. Those people could include members of the group you're playing with, or the group ahead of you, or workers on the course maintenance crew. Regardless, it's the player's responsibility to make sure the area ahead is clear so that no one gets hurt.

Remember that the golf ball doesn't always head toward the intended target; golfers occasionally mis-hit the ball and send it way off-line. People standing even significantly off to either side of the target line are at risk of being struck and injured by a wayward shot. Therefore, it's important to stay *behind* the golfer who is playing, to assure that you can't get hit by a ball. In the rare and unfortunate cases where you are responsible for hitting a ball off-line, please immediately yell "Fore!" to alert anyone in the possible landing zone. And if you hear "Fore!" yelled out, turn *away* from that direction, and try to protect your head and neck.

The Golf Cart

Many golf courses assume that everyone knows how to drive a golf cart. Most facilities do require a driver's license, but it's the player's responsibility to know how to operate the cart. Frankly, it's not that difficult; but if it's your first time, you should inform the facility. It would be wise to take a few minutes to read the instructions that are posted on the vehicle and head to a less-populated area to get comfortable with the controls. Other important notes: Try to keep the cart on designated cart paths when possible. Do not attempt to drive on steep hills. Always engage the parking (locking) brake before leaving the vehicle. Keep your hands and feet inside the cart at all times. Obey signage on the golf course; there may be signs that instruct you where to travel.

Weather

In heavy rain, gloves, grips, and the ground can get slippery. Take extra caution when swinging the club in these conditions. Make sure to take practice swings to check your footing, and be careful that the club doesn't slip and fly out of your hands. Rainy weather can be managed, but *never* play golf when there's a chance of electricity in the air. Lightning is a serious threat, and in open spaces and with metal clubs in their hands, golfers are dangerously exposed. If a storm rolls in while you're playing, get in your cart and immediately head to the clubhouse or a safe structure (no, a big tree is not a safe structure).

etiquette

Golf is a game of integrity, in which players are expected to be honest and abide by the rules during competition. Additionally, golfers should take care to respect other players and the golf course. Beginners may be unaware of proper golf etiquette and expected sportsmanship. Here I've listed several golf course scenarios, along with appropriate protocol. Following these guidelines will show fellow players that you're courteous, considerate, and you understand how golf should be played.

Who Swings First?

On the first tee, the order of play is random. It will sometimes be determined by drawing straws, flipping a tee to the ground (and seeing who it points to), flipping a coin, or just asking "Who's ready?" But once the group has teed off, the order is very defined. The player who is farthest from the hole will be the first to play. This routine continues even on the putting green, and until everyone has holed out. At the next tee, the player with the lowest score from the previous hole has "the honor" and will tee off first. If scores are the same, then you maintain the order of play from the previous tee.

Stay Quiet

Show consideration by remaining quiet and relatively still while other players are in their address position and preparing to swing. Loud noises and excessive movement can be distracting, and are frowned upon.

No Cell Phones

Some facilities will not allow any use of cell phones or other electronic devices during play or practice. But even if allowed, it's very important to turn off the sound on your phone! A quick text may be okay, but allowing your phone to ring or having an audible phone conversation is considered very rude.

Tipping

Tipping policies differ from club to club. The best thing to do is ask about tipping during your initial phone call to the facility. Regardless of the answer, I've found it is always best to have some small bills at the ready. Caddie tips are fairly standard, but you may also want to tip the locker room attendant, an outside staffer who cleans your clubs after the round, the caddie master if he goes out of his way to assist you, a valet who may park your car, etc. Obviously, not all golf facilities offer service positions that warrant such gratuities. But it's always best to be prepared.

Pace of Play

One of the most annoying issues in golf is slow play. Other golfers don't care what your score is, but they do care if you play slowly. The best rule of thumb is to keep up with the group in front of you. If you notice you're slowing down the other players in your group, or other players behind you on the course, here are some suggestions:

1. Don't wait until it's your turn to start thinking about your shot. You should choose your club and be prepared to play *before* it's your turn to swing.

2. You could simply speed up your normal routine a bit: walk faster, take fewer practice swings, etc.

3. Pick up your ball. If you're really struggling on a hole, it's okay to pick up the ball, take a breather, and try again at the next hole (provided you're not in an official tournament that requires you to finish every hole).

4. If nothing seems to work, and there are people waiting to play behind you, let them through! It's always proper etiquette to let faster players pass you on the course. Simply step to the side and motion them to "come on through." Once they've passed you and are well out of range, continue your game—but try to keep up with them.

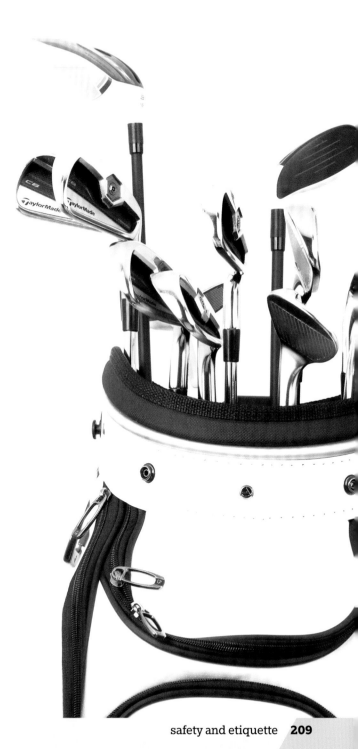

On the Green

Be careful not to step on the ground between another player's ball and the hole. This is called "stepping on someone's line of putt," and should be avoided. You should also be wary of your shadow—it can be distracting to other players. Make sure your shadow does not interfere with another golfer's stroke or line of play.

The Flagstick

When all golf balls from your group are on the green, the flagstick should be carefully removed and gently placed on the ground. Never throw or slam it on the ground, and always place it off the green or far from any chance of being struck by a ball.

The Cart

Never drive or park your cart on a putting green or a teeing ground. Make sure your golf cart is never within 10 yards (9 meters) of the putting surface.

Your Golf Bag

If you are carrying your bag, be sure to put it down on ground surrounding the green. It should not interfere with the swing or play of another golfer, and you should never put your golf bag on the putting surface.

Replacing Divots

A divot is a chunk of turf that is ripped from the ground after a shot. Always take the time to replace your divots. After taking a shot, find that chunk of turf, carefully replace it in the bare spot that was created, and press it firmly into place with your foot. If you can't find the divot, or it explodes into many pieces, fill the bare spot with divot mix and smooth it out with your foot. Divot mix is a combination of sand, soil, and seed. Divot mix containers can usually be found on golf carts or in a container near a par-3 teeing ground.

Repairing Ball Marks and Spike Marks

When you hit a nice approach shot that hits the green, the ball usually leaves a ball mark—a concave depression in the putting surface. Before you putt, it's important to take a tee or a ball mark repair tool and fix that mark. Insert the tee or repair tool into the turf at several points surrounding the depression, and gently twist or push toward the center until the putting surface is perfectly flat again. If there are additional ball or spike marks others have failed to repair, take an extra second or two and fix them as well!

Raking the Bunker

Hitting a ball into a bunker can be frustrating, but finding your ball sitting in the bottom of someone's sandy footprint is frustrating at a much higher level. If you play a shot from the sand, it's your responsibility to rake that sand as you leave the bunker. It's common golf courtesy to leave the bunker sand smooth; no footprints or divot holes should be visible if you've raked correctly. When finished, place the rake back where you found it. Some courses prefer to leave rakes in the sand, others leave them outside the bunker.

General Behavior

It probably goes without saying that cursing, abusing the course, and/or angry club-throwing are all extremely inappropriate actions. Such embarrassing behavior is unacceptable. Yes, golf can be frustrating at times, but always maintain composure. Treat the course and your equipment with respect and react to difficult situations and poor shots with class. Win or lose, smile and shake hands with your fellow players (and caddies if you have them) at the end of your round. Conduct yourself with dignity and others will be eager to play golf with you again—act like an idiot, and you'll have a hard time finding a game.

different ways to play the game

Most people who are interested in golf but have never truly played think only of the game they see on television. Golf tournaments that are shown on TV usually feature the Stroke Play format. Individual Stroke Play is the most challenging format, because players are required to keep track of every single swing they make. Each stroke is added up, and the total score at the end of 18 holes is posted. It's certainly the most common format, but not necessarily the most enjoyable style of play for a beginner! Fortunately, there's a wide variety of golf games—and many of them are far less stressful than Stroke Play.

One of the great things about golf is that you can play with a partner against the two other players in your group, your foursome can play together as a team, or you can even play alone against the course. Regardless, there are countless styles of play that vary from loose, fun, and social to very challenging and competitive. One of the unique qualities of golf is that with the proper format, players of different skill levels can play with, and even compete against, each other evenly.

In addition to describing the more common styles of play, I will introduce you to a number of other golf formats that are likely to be more enjoyable for the beginner. These different golf games take the pressure off and can elevate enjoyment, even for the seasoned player. I encourage you to mix it up and try some different formats. The variety of options adds another level of interest to this great sport!

common formats of play

Individual Stroke Play

Also known as Medal Play, this is the most common format, and the format that most Professional Tour events utilize. Quite simply, each player records the total number of strokes he or she takes on each of the 18 holes. After adding all the strokes together, the 18-hole total is posted. If the tournament consists of four 18-hole rounds, the scores from each round are added together for a 72-hole total. The player who needs the fewest number of strokes to complete the designated number of holes is the winner.

Individual Match Play

Although slightly less popular these days, Match Play has been around for centuries. Unlike Stroke Play, in Match Play you only have one opponent. The two of you tee off on the first hole, and the player who requires the fewest number of strokes to complete the hole will be "one up." It doesn't matter whether the score was 4 to 5 or 4 to 9, the player who scored the 4 is one up—or leading the match by one hole. If you both score the same, the hole is "halved," or tied. This format requires a different type of strategy. If your opponent hits a ball in the water, you may decide to play safe, but if your partner hits his shot close to the hole, you know you'll have to be aggressive. Match Play is sometimes preferred by players who normally have a few very high scores on holes during a round. The round theoretically consists of 18 chances to win a hole. The player to win the most holes will be the winner.

Four-Ball Stroke Play

In this "better ball of partners" format, you team up with another golfer and play against the other two players in your foursome, as well as all the other two-person teams in the event. Each player plays their ball like a normal Stroke Play event, but only the better score of the two teammates is recorded. Since only one score counts, the strategy can be a bit different. If your partner hits a safe shot to the middle of the green, then you can be more aggressive and try to attack the flag. But if your partner hits his ball in the water, you had better play a bit safer because your score will likely be the score that counts for your team. This format generally keeps play moving along at a quicker pace because individual scores are not as important. If your partner is in good shape and you just took your third swing to try to escape the bunker, you can simply pick up your ball and go to the next hole, since your partner has you covered.

Four-Ball Match Play

Four-Ball Match Play is a team event where two players form a team or side that plays against another two-player team. Both players on the team play their own ball, and the better ball of one team is matched against the better ball of the other team. The team with the lower score wins the hole; ties are halved. The team who wins the most holes out of 18 is declared the winning team.

Alternate Shot

This is a Stroke Play event that is typically played with one partner, but only one ball is used for the team. Both players tee off, and the best shot of the two is chosen. The player who did not hit the chosen shot will play the second shot, and they will alternate until the ball is holed. The player who knocks in the putt on the first hole will not tee off on the next hole, but will hit the second shot on that hole. That alternating style continues through the 18 holes with only the one ball. Any penalty strokes that take place will not change the order of play.

Another version of this format is called Alternate Shot, Alternate Teeing Ground, where player A on the team tees off on all the odd-numbered holes, and player B tees off on all the even-numbered holes. Alternating strokes with the one ball occurs throughout the round, but the tee-shot assignments have been pre-determined.

Pinehurst

Pinehurst is a form of Alternate Shot that allows both members of a two-person team to tee off on each of the 18 holes of the match. The ball in the best position after the tee shots becomes the chosen ball in play. The team alternates shots with this ball until it's holed, starting with the team member who didn't hit the drive with the chosen ball.

Chapman

The Chapman format is also a form of Alternate Shot. Chapman involves a team of two players (A and B). They both tee off, but then A switches and plays his second shot with B's ball, and B plays A's ball. After the second shots have been struck, the players choose the ball that's in the best position. The team then alternates shots with that one ball until the ball is holed.

Best Ball of Four

This format brings all four members of a foursome together as a team. The pressure is lower in this format because you have four players each playing their own ball, but only the lowest score for each hole is recorded. This is a great social event where the score for your team is up against all the other foursomes in the tournament. If a player is struggling, he or she is encouraged to pick up their ball on that particular hole and let their partners get a good score for the team. Because struggling players can pick up, this format moves along at a nice pace. Although this very popular format is not listed in the second category, it's a very good game for beginners. A more challenging version is Two Best Balls of Four, where the two best of the four scores on each hole are added together and recorded for the team.

The Shamble

The Shamble is usually played as a team of four event. All four players tee off, and the best drive of the four is chosen. The other three players bring their ball to the spot where the best tee shot lies, and all four players then play all the way into the cup from that spot. The best score of the four will count for the team.

Stableford

Stableford is a format that awards points based on a player's score on each hole. A common scale for accumulating points with this system: bogey = 1 point, par = 2 points, birdie = 3 points, eagle = 4 points, and double eagle = 5 points. This format can be used for either team or individual play. In a Stableford competition, the player with the highest point total wins. Since any score above bogey (or designated score) is 0, players can pick up if they're struggling and on their way to a high score for a particular hole. This format will move along fairly quickly.

Skins

In this format, each hole is worth a designated amount of points or money. Let's say, for example, that each hole is worth $1. The four (or fewer) golfers each play the hole with their own ball. The lowest or best score on the hole wins the dollar! If there's a tie for the low score on the hole, then a "carry-over" takes place. The money from that first hole gets carried over or added to the next hole, making the second hole worth $2. It's a fun game that doesn't require a player to keep track of every single stroke he or she takes.

A quick note on wagering: Betting is a common practice on the golf course. If you enjoy a little "action" or additional pressure, be sure to have extra money in your pocket. A few words of advice: Make sure you know the details of the wager before you hit your first shot. Never bet beyond your comfort level, and if you're uncomfortable at all with wagering, you can just respectfully decline to be a part of the bet.

great games for beginners

The Scramble

The Scramble is a fun and very social format that's frequently used in large golf outings. Each foursome is a team. All players in the group hit tee shots. The best position of those shots is chosen, and all players hit their next shots from that point. The best of those shots is chosen, and all players then play their third shots from that point, and so on. That process continues (even on the putting green) until the ball is holed. One variation of the Scramble requires that three (or one, two, or four) tee shots from each player must be selected and used as the team's shot. This adds a layer of strategy and pressure, especially if there's only one hole left and a player has only used two of his tee shots. He will probably feel a bit nervous on that last tee knowing that his tee shot is the one that must be selected!

Individual Two-Ball Scramble

Some golf courses have rules prohibiting a golfer from playing more than one ball at a time, but if the course is okay with it, and you are not slowing down the pace or interfering with others, this is a great game. The concept is simple: an individual hits two balls off the tee, chooses the better of the two shots, and then plays two shots from that point. The routine continues, even with putting, until the ball is holed. You basically get two chances at each spot you play from. The Two-Ball Scramble is a great way to ease in to playing golf. Two players could even play this format, but that would be the limit—a group shouldn't have more than four golf balls in play.

Make Your Own Course

Most courses have various tee-markers to choose from based on skill level and experience. But even the shortest set of tee-markers may be too much for a true beginner. Rather than play from the forward tees, some beginners should consider teeing up for their first shot at the 150 yard (137m) mark on each hole. They would play the forward tees on all the par 3s, but tee up 150 yards from the green on all the par 4s and 5s. This will make the course much shorter. It's a great way to get comfortable playing golf. As the beginner grows more confident, he or she can move back to the 200 yard (183m) mark. Soon they'll be comfortable playing from the forward tees.

Ringers

Ringers is really tracking a golfer's "personal best." For example, a player keeps the scorecard from the first time he plays a course. Each time he plays that same course in the future, he tries to better his score on each hole. If his score on a particular hole is lower than his previous best, he adjusts his personal best scorecard. It's fun to see the best hole-by-hole scores you've produced at a certain golf facility over the course of a season.

Bingle, Bangle, Bungle

This is a fun format that has very little to do with traditional scorekeeping. In Bingle, Bangle, Bungle, there are three points available on each hole. The first point is awarded to the first player in the group who lands (and keeps) his ball on the green (remember the player who is farthest from the hole always plays first). The next point goes to the player who is closest to the hole once all balls are on the putting surface—it doesn't matter how many strokes it took to get there. The third point goes to the player who holes his ball first (no "tap-ins" or "gimmees"; farthest from the hole always plays first). You can award a financial value to each point, or simply add up all player points at the end of the round. The player with the highest point total wins.

Closest to Every Pin

Rather than focus entirely on the number of strokes needed to complete 18 holes, Closest to Every Pin gives a point to the player whose ball is closest to the cup once every ball in the group is on the green. It may take an experienced player two shots to reach the putting surface, while a less-experienced player needs four or five. How many it takes to get there is not the concern with this game—only who is closer once all balls are on the green. This format offers 18 different chances to win and is fun to play when golfers in a group vary significantly in skill level.

Fewest Putts

Similar to Closest to Every Pin, Fewest Putts is not concerned with how many strokes are required to reach the green. In this format, the player with the fewest number of putts needed to hole out on all 18 greens wins. Better players may reach the green sooner, but are often farther from the hole than a player who misses the green and chips it close. This is a simple format that focuses on the importance of good putting, and allows players of all skill levels to compete fairly evenly.

One Club

The rules allow a player to carry 14 different clubs for a round of golf. One Club is a very interesting format that requires players to choose only one club for their entire round. Obviously, great care needs to be taken on the greens (if you're putting with a 7-iron, for example), and you must remember to repair divots on all teeing grounds. But One Club can make for an interesting variation of golf. This format forces players to work on adjusting their swings for different situations. It can actually help players become more creative and think strategically while playing golf.

Junk

Junk is a game that rewards various achievements on a golf hole, and frankly, you can customize your own point system to keep the entire round interesting. For example:

Greenie: a point for being closest to the pin after hitting the green.

Sandie: hitting your ball out of a sand bunker, and then holing out the next shot.

Birdie: (could be par, or even bogey, depending on the skill level of the group) rewarding a certain score relative to par.

Fairway: a point for hitting the fairway off the tee.

Up and Down: a point for hitting a shot on the green and then making the putt.

Chip-In: a point for chipping in from off the green.

Barkie: a point for making par after hitting a tree with your ball at some point during the play of the hole.

Three-Putt: subtract a point for 3-putting.

These are just a few examples of junk points. Make up your own system—just make sure everyone understands the points before you start the round. Junk can be added to many of the other formats, and it sure keeps golfers interested throughout the round. Even if they're not playing that well, they can always make a great shot and get rewarded! Junk can add some fun to your game!

Hopefully this chapter has given you some new perspective. In addition to the traditional forms of play, there are many different ways to enjoy and challenge yourself on the golf course. Yes, I think it's important to work toward a level where you can keep track of all the strokes you've taken and post an official score. But it might take a little time until you're comfortable playing a regulation Stroke Play round of golf. In the meantime, try some formats that are fun and challenging for players of all levels—and don't be surprised if that seasoned player in your group enjoys a different style of play as well!

taking it a step further

the golf handicap

Can you imagine walking onto the basketball court for a game of one-on-one against Michael Jordan? How about stepping into the ring to box with Mike Tyson for a few rounds? My guess is that neither matchup would be very competitive (and the Tyson match would quickly lead you to the nearest hospital). But one of the great things about golf is that players of differing ability levels can compete evenly against one another. A relative beginner can have a fun and very competitive match against Tiger Woods! Golf can actually create a fair contest between an expert and a beginner through the use of the United States Golf Association's handicap system.

In this chapter, I'll explain how the handicap system works and why it helps to make golf more enjoyable for everyone. I'll also help you understand how handicaps are used in a few common situations on the course. Once you understand the many benefits, you'll certainly want an official USGA handicap of your own.

what is a handicap?

In very general terms, an official handicap is a number that represents a player's skill and potential scoring ability, and gives a fair indication of what scores a player can be expected to shoot. The lower the handicap number, the better the player. While player A, with a 36 handicap, might shoot 110 for 18 holes, player B, with a 0 handicap (also known as a "scratch" player), may shoot a 72. The number of strokes a golfer actually takes for 18 holes is known as the *gross score.*

Handicaps for Stroke Play Events (Gross vs. Net)

The gross score minus the player's handicap equals the *net score.* For example, in the case of the scores above, player A shot a gross 110 minus a course handicap of 36 for a net 74. And player B shot a gross 72 minus a course handicap of 0, for a net 72.

This example shows two golfers subtracting course handicaps from gross scores to arrive at a total net score, but a handicap match can also be set up in a different way.

Handicaps for Match Play Events

Match Play events are less concerned with total score, and focus on winning, losing, or halving (tying) each hole, and the handicap system can make this form of play very fair as well.

Every course ranks its holes according to difficulty, from easiest (the #18 hdcp hole) to most difficult (the #1 hdcp hole). On the scorecard you'll notice this ranking number next to each hole—for example, hole #1 may be the #7 hdcp hole, or the seventh most difficult hole on the course. This ranking of difficulty by hole is important when playing a handicapped match against an opponent of a different skill level. For example, in a match between a player with a 20 hdcp and a player with an 18 hdcp, the 18 hdcp has a skill advantage of two strokes. To make the match fair, the 20 hdcp will subtract one stroke from his score on each of the two most difficult holes.

Handicaps can be used in a wide variety of golf events and competitions, and I strongly recommend applying for an official USGA handicap.

How to Get a Handicap Index, and How It Converts to a Course Handicap

Official handicaps are not given directly to individuals. They are issued through licensed golf clubs and facilities that adhere to the policies and procedures of the USGA handicapping system. Most golf facilities are set up in this system. If you aren't a member of a club, simply go to your local public golf course and ask to sign up for a handicap. There will be a small annual fee, but you can quickly sign up and begin the process. Once you're in the system, you will be assigned a member number, which you will use to sign in. After entering five 18-hole scores (or ten 9-hole scores) you will be given a handicap index.

The handicap index is a number with a decimal (for example 18.6) that can be used at any golf course. The index is converted to a course handicap by using a conversion chart that can be found at each golf course. The more difficult the course, the higher the handicap you will be given. For example, at a relatively easy course with very few hazards, an 18.6 might convert to a course handicap of 16. But at a very long, challenging course, that same 18.6 might convert to a 22. The index is even likely to change depending on which set of tees you play from at a given course. The whole idea of a handicap is to maintain an accurate measure of your golfing abilities. The system works like a charm, and will produce an accurate handicap as long as you do two simple things:

1. Try your best on every hole you play.

2. Enter or post every score you shoot (not just the good scores, and not just the bad scores—all of them).

Some players keep track of all their results and simply average their scores to arrive at a "score they usually shoot." That routine will not lead to an accurate handicap, and such calculations are not official. Due to the fact that courses vary dramatically in length and levels of difficulty, the universal USGA handicap formula is the best way to go.

Course Rating and Slope Rating

The *course rating* is a number with one decimal place (for example 71.4), indicating the likely score of a scratch (or zero handicap) golfer at a given course under normal conditions. This rating is based on many different difficulty factors, such as length of course, width of fairways, impact of hazards, etc. The *slope rating* of a course is a calculated number that indicates how difficult the course is for the average player. The higher the slope, the more difficult a golf course is. The easiest course would have a rating of 55, while the most difficult rating available is 155; the average course has a slope rating of 113. On courses with higher course ratings and slope ratings, your handicap index would convert to a higher course handicap.

GlenArbor Golf Club

U.S.G.A RULES GOVERN PLAY

MENS RATINGS		WOMENS RATINGS	
BLACK:	74.1 / 145	WHITE:	75.1 / 139
BLUE:	72.4 / 139	GREEN:	72.2 / 130
PLAYER:	71.2 / 137		
WHITE:	69.7 / 132		

Bedford, New York

Other Uses for an Official Handicap

In addition to providing a means for fair competition among players of various skill levels, handicaps are also required if you plan to play in club events and many other tournaments. Also, a handicap is a great indicator of improvement. As your game (and your scoring) improves, your handicap index will slowly drop. The system automatically updates every two weeks, and if your ability level changes, your index will reflect improvement (or a lack thereof). After reading this book, your scores are sure to lower. And as you enter better scores, your handicap will begin to drop—the official handicap is a fun way to chart your progress!

As I mentioned earlier, you should head to your local public golf facility and begin the process of obtaining an official handicap. Some people are reluctant, and feel that they should be comfortable with their swing before getting a handicap. I strongly disagree! Take the first step now, and enjoy the process of measuring your improvement. You don't even need to go to the course to access your handicap information. You can access, input, and review information online at www.GHIN.com. You can also learn much more about the handicap system at www.usga.org.

Handicap vs. Handicap Index

A lot of times the terms "handicap" and "handicap index" are used interchangeably—but do they mean the same thing? Technically, no. In general terms, your handicap is what you typically shoot, minus par. Your handicap index is a number (with a decimal) that is calculated based on the scores you enter into the USGA (or other governing body) Handicap System. Your handicap index is an accurate indication of your golfing ability, and that number is a constant. That handicap index is then applied to the golf course you're playing, and since courses vary in difficulty, your handicap will vary as well.

improving your game

We've all heard the saying "practice makes perfect." Well, I hate to burst your bubble, but "perfect" doesn't exist in golf! Golf involves changing weather conditions, differing course conditions, and a wide variety of factors that are far beyond our control. This great sport will never be mastered.

You will feel the sheer joy of a perfect shot, and roll in some perfect putts, but each imperfect shot leaves us with a chance for an exciting recovery. Embrace and enjoy the challenge! And welcome the fact that since golf is never perfect, you can always improve. Practice is certainly an important step in the right direction!

Practicing is great, but practicing *properly* is far more productive. Going to the driving range, taking out your driver, and pounding buckets of balls into oblivion is *not* the answer. In this chapter, I will discuss the factors that lead to successful practice, and outline the key elements of an effective program. We'll also look at finding an instructor, if you would like to go that route. Spending your practice time wisely will lead you to better scores and more enjoyment on the golf course.

10 steps for improving your game

1. **Assess your game.** Ideally, you can meet with a PGA golf instructor who will assess your swing and help you develop a plan for improvement. Another way to assess your game is to keep track of your performance on the course. Record the number of putts you take during a round. Mark down the number of fairways you hit off the tee and the number of greens you hit in regulation. Keeping track of this data can help you see which areas of your game need the most improvement.

2. **Work on your fundamentals.** Even the best players in the world continue to work on their grip, posture, and address positions. Never underestimate the importance of a solid setup. Make sure your grip is comfortable and consistent. Check your posture in a full-length mirror and make sure you're starting your swing from a great position. Always set up an alignment station when you practice. Having alignment rods or two extra clubs to indicate a parallel address, a square clubface, and an awareness of your target is very valuable!

3. **Simplify your thoughts.** Don't try to get everything done in one session. You should work on one specific area that needs improving. Additionally, you need to focus on only one or two swing thoughts. Golfers who address the ball with a laundry list of multiple thoughts are heading for serious frustration. Ideally, commit to one key thought or goal for your swing—don't get clouded with too many ideas.

4. **Use targets and visualization.** Many driving ranges have multiple targets to help you aim your shots. If the range doesn't have obvious targets, then find some of your own (a yardage sign, a pole or tree at the side of the range, a house in the distance, a discolored area of turf, etc.). By using specific targets at the range, your practice becomes more like playing on a golf course. Change targets often, and try to visualize your ball heading to the target before you even swing. This form of a pre-shot routine will be a huge help and will transfer nicely to the golf course!

5. **Swing for quality, not quantity.** It's very important to have a clear thought process, rehearse with practice swings, and take your time visualizing successful results prior to each shot. Too many golfers get lost on the range and just make one swing after another without much thought. They've hit tons of balls, the bucket is empty, but they haven't made any progress. Take your time! Hit fewer balls, but make them count. You might try getting a smaller bucket and taking more time in between shots.

6. **Create your own competitions.** Set goals for yourself during practice sessions. An example might be to land 4 shots out of 10 on a set target. When you reach that goal, try for 5. Another goal may be hitting your target three times in a row—can you get to four? Succeeding under these circumstances will lead to better results on the golf course.

7. **Switch it up and play "the course" on the range.** How often do you hit 25 straight 7-irons while playing golf on the course? Never! Try this great practice technique: Toward the end of your session, hit shots as if you were playing your favorite course. Visualize the opening tee shot. Pick the club you would use and play the shot as if you were there. Then wait a bit and hit your next shot while visualizing the second shot at that course. The first shot might have been with a driver, the second with a wedge, the third full swing might be with a 3-wood (if that's the club you would use off the second tee), and so on. "Playing" an imaginary course and constantly switching clubs for different shots will simulate your activity on an actual golf course and better prepare you for golf.

8. **Work on your short game.** Few golfers spend enough time working on their chipping, pitching, and putting. Most shots on the golf course take place from only 100 yards (91m) away from the flag or closer. Yet most golfers spend the overwhelming majority of their practice time working on full swings and bombing drives. The more comfortable you become with your putting and those smaller shots around the green, the better you will score!

9. **Use training aids.** Using training aids that are appropriate for your swing improvement plan can also be helpful. But beware! Using the wrong devices (or even using the proper aids in the wrong way) can be detrimental. It would be wise to have a PGA professional confirm that a particular training aid is appropriate for you, and even help you to devise a plan to use it effectively. Remember, successful swings come in many shapes and sizes. A gadget that might help your friend's swing could be damaging to yours.

10. **Stay positive.** Practicing properly will lead to a much better game, but you need to be patient and set realistic goals. If you try too hard, or expect too much too soon, you might get frustrated. Savor the great shots and learn from the bad ones—a positive approach always works best. Enjoy your journey to a better game!

finding an instructor

Yes, golf is fun, and players tend to enjoy the game even more as they improve. Practicing will help you become a better golfer, but practicing *correctly* will improve your game quicker and take you to the next level of success! The best plan of action for a golfer who wants to improve is to find a qualified instructor. A PGA professional can give you the individual attention and insight to get the most out of your swing. A PGA pro can also help you prepare a game plan for improvement, prescribe drills to work on, and teach you to practice more effectively.

Where to Look

There are countless golf facilities across the country—private, public, and resort courses, driving ranges, and even certain sporting goods stores—that have golf instructors on-site. Finding a golf instructor is not hard—but finding the *right* golf instructor might take a little research. The first step in the process would be to ask friends or acquaintances who play golf if there is a PGA instructor they would recommend. You may prefer a female professional, one who has a certain level of expertise, or perhaps an instructor who specializes in one area of the game.

Professionals who have received awards, are published or featured on television, or have a proven track record with PGA Tour players often come with a higher price tag. But you will find a number of different price levels.

There are also PGA assistant professionals and apprentices who are very good teachers but lack years of experience, and are therefore available at a lower rate. You could also consider taking a lesson with a friend or two and dividing the cost accordingly. Some facilities offer group clinics and special promotions that allow you to receive great advice at a fraction of the cost. But to be honest, nothing is better than a one-on-one lesson with a great instructor.

A referral from someone you trust is invaluable, but you can also go to www.pga.com, click on "Improve Your Game," and then click "Find a Coach." The site will give a list of fully certified PGA professionals in your area of the country after you type in your location.

Check Out the Pro

Once you have some names or well-respected facilities to choose from, I would advise you to speak with the instructors personally (and even Google them if you have the chance). The introductory conversation and background check is an interview of sorts. PGA instructors are all well trained and know the swing inside and out, but it's more important to find a pro who can communicate comfortably with you. The best instructors are those who help identify your goals, help you create a program for improvement, and have a style and personality that suits you.

Lessons are usually available in 30-, 45-, or 60-minute segments, and some instructors offer a lesson package (where you might pay up front for five or six lessons) that gives you a discounted price. I would recommend taking a half-hour lesson to start off, and make sure you like the instructor's style and delivery before committing to a series of lessons.

Playing lessons, or on-course instruction, can also be an option. Playing golf on an actual course while under the watchful eye of a PGA instructor is a very valuable experience. The instructor can see how you truly perform during the "heat of battle," and can offer technical advice as well as course management strategies.

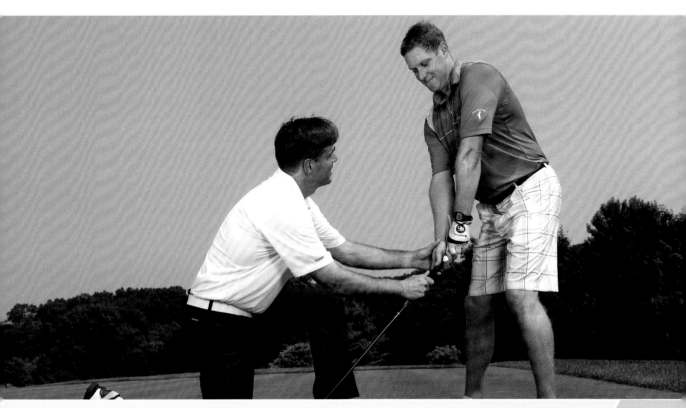

Preparing for Your Lesson

It's important to be prepared for your golf lesson. You should be able to articulate your goals, and also indicate how much time you will realistically have for future instruction, practice, and rounds of play. You should also find out about the dress code, and ask if there are clubs you can use or if you need to bring your own. If you enjoy learning visually, you might prefer a facility with video analysis equipment. If video instruction is important to you, be sure to ask if it's available. Always arrive at the facility early so you can find your way around, and loosen up a bit before the lesson starts.

I've heard beginners say, "I'm not good or consistent enough to take a lesson—I'll wait until I'm better." Frankly, this doesn't make much sense. Don't wait! Have a golf professional assist with your improvement at an early stage if possible—it will help you find a greater level of golfing enjoyment!

Golf Schools

I've mentioned individual lessons and clinics, but golf schools are also available. Often associated with well-known golf destinations and resorts, golf schools specialize in group instruction, which make many beginners feel more comfortable. These schools are available in one-day, multiple-day, or even weeklong sessions, and are typically very structured, with a pretty intense schedule—you learn a lot of content in that very concentrated period of time. In most schools you get serious attention from a PGA professional staff, a specific learning agenda, and some free time to play golf at the facility courses, as well as reference materials for you to take home. Many schools also feature a lecture format where students can take notes and ask questions. I would do some research and get feedback before deciding on a particular school, and I strongly recommend a school that features PGA professional instruction. Be sure to get positive testimonials before attending a school, too.

There are dozens—perhaps hundreds—of golf schools and clinics around the world, and choosing one can be an overwhelming task. Here is a list of beautiful clubs and resorts that often host reputable golf schools staffed by PGA professionals. For more options, check out *Golf Digest* magazine's annual list of best golf schools and academies.

The Ritz-Carlton and JW Marriott at Grand Lakes
Orlando, Florida

The Westin Diplomat Resort & Spa
Hollywood, Florida

Chardonnay Golf Club
Napa, California

The Westin Mission Hills
Palm Desert, California

Amelia Island Plantation
Amelia Island, Florida

Raptor Bay Golf Club
Naples, Florida

Pebble Beach Resorts
Pebble Beach, California

Royal Links Golf Club
Las Vegas, Nevada

The Westin Kierland Golf Club
Scottsdale, Arizona

Talking Stick Golf Club
Scottsdale, Arizona

Four Seasons Troon North Resort & Spa
Scottsdale, Arizona

Kiawah Island Golf Resort
Kiawah, South Carolina

Longboat Key Club & Resort
Sarasota, Florida

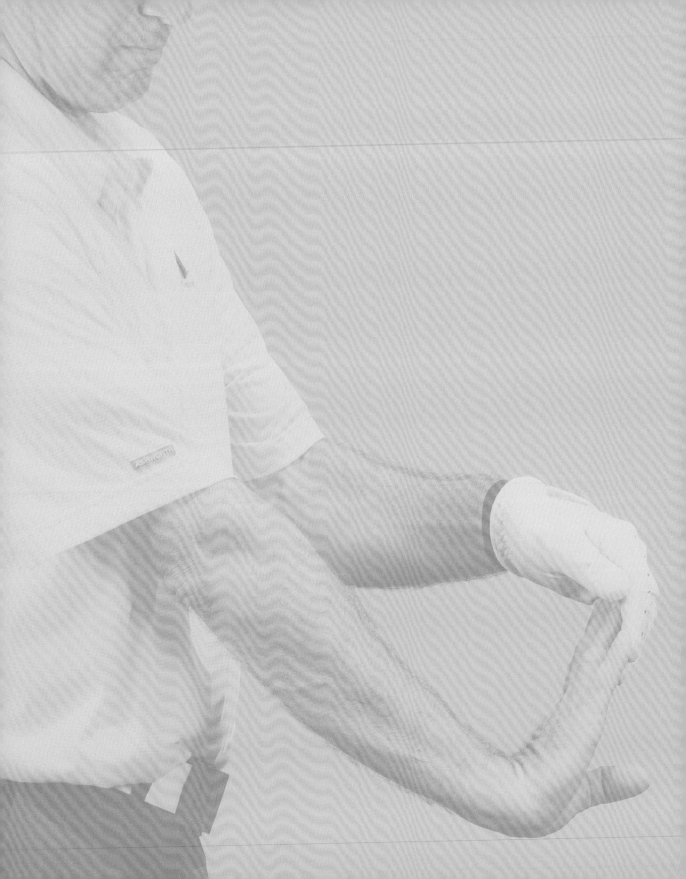

fitness and wellness

Do you need to be in top physical condition to play a great game of golf? Absolutely not. But increasing your strength, flexibility, and stamina can truly improve your game—and the rest of your life, for that matter. Assuming you're in reasonable shape, it's still very important to warm up properly before your round.

There are very comprehensive programs that are designed to target your golfing muscles and train you specifically for a better golf swing. I'm not going to take you to that level, but this chapter will offer some helpful pre-round stretches that can help prevent injury and prepare you for a pain-free day on the course, and some tips on keeping yourself healthy throughout the game.

simple warm-up stretches

First of all, you should make every effort to arrive at the course early enough to warm up properly. It's very common for golfers to screech into the parking lot and run to the first tee without doing a single stretch or taking a single practice swing. Get to the course at least 30 minutes before you're scheduled to tee off, and perform some of the following stretches.

Knee Bends

Don't let your knees come out over your toes.

1. Hold a club in front of you, one hand toward each end, with your feet shoulder-width apart.

2. Slowly lower yourself by bending at the knees and waist, as if you're going to sit in a chair. Go down only as far as is comfortable, but the goal is to bend your knees to at least a 90-degree angle.

3. Slowly come back up to the starting position by pressing your weight into your heels and pushing up.

4. Lower and rise six to seven times.

Keep the club parallel to the ground throughout the entire movement.

Waist Twists

Keep the club parallel to the ground throughout the entire movement.

Keep your knees facing forward–you should only be moving your torso here.

1. Hold a club in front of you and stand with your feet shoulder-width apart, knees slightly flexed, and your back straight.

2. Slowly twist from the waist 90 degrees to the right. Hold that position for a count of five.

3. Return to face forward, keeping the club in front of you.

4. Repeat the twist on the left side, holding for a count of five. Return to the front position.

5. Repeat this process six to seven times.

Shoulder Stretch

1. Place your right hand on top of your driver clubhead, and hold the grip end with your left. Bring the grip in near your waist.

2. Relax the raised arm, slowly push upward on the club with your left hand until you feel resistance on the upper arm, and feel the stretch in your shoulder and back.

3. When you can stretch no farther, hold that position for a count of five.

4. Relax the stretch, and bring the club down.

5. Switch hand positions so that the left hand is at the top and the right is on the grip. Repeat the stretch on the other side.

6. Stretch each side three to four times.

Golf is a great form of exercise, provided you opt to walk instead of drive around in a cart. In fact, if you were to walk a typical golf course, you would be walking close to 5 miles (8km) over uneven terrain. That may not qualify as an intense workout, but it sure is better than sitting on the couch and watching your third straight hour of television!

Quad Stretch

Be sure to keep your back straight.

Don't let your knee come out over your toes–keep it aligned with your heel.

1. Begin in a standing position with legs together. Bring one leg back behind you, keeping your front leg straight.

2. Place both hands on the knee of your forward leg for support, and start to slowly lower yourself down, bending at the knee with the forward leg.

3. Press the heel of your back leg into the ground as much as you can, to get a good stretch.

4. Hold the post for a count of five, and then slowly come back up, straightening your front leg.

5. Come back to a standing position, bringing your back leg forward.

6. Repeat the exercise on the opposite side. Stretch each side three to four times.

Wrist Stretch

Make sure all four fingers are supported by your "pressing" hand–don't just pull on the tips of your fingers.

1. Hold your right arm out in front of you with your hand and fingers pointed upward.

2. Place your left hand on the fingertips of your right, palm facing toward you, fingers pointing down. Press into your right hand, slowly pulling back on those vertical fingers. You will feel the stretch in your right wrist.

3. Keep pulling back until you feel resistance, hold the position for a count of five, and release.

4. Switch and do the same stretch on the opposite side.

5. Stretch each wrist three to four times.

Warming Up Your Swing

As a finish to your warm-up routine, I recommend taking some relaxing swings while holding two clubs. Swing in both directions while maintaining good posture and balance–just as you would with a regular swing.

Once you've done that, go to one club and hit several shots with relaxed, three-quarter swings—don't swing at 100 percent right away. This will release tension, loosen your muscles, and get your thoughts straight for the upcoming round.

If you only plan on practicing, the exact pre-round routine should take place prior to beginning your practice session. This warm-up and stretching session should help you avoid unnecessary injury while playing or practicing golf.

Be careful of practicing excessively on artificial mats (which are sometimes installed on top of crushed stone, asphalt, or concrete). Practicing for extended periods of time on these hard surfaces can lead to injury—especially in areas with cold weather.

additional health and wellness considerations

Stretching isn't the only thing you need to be concerned about when it comes to preparing for a round of golf. Here are some other things to consider before you get onto the course.

Snacks

A round of golf can take more than four hours—and your body is likely to need some fuel during that span of time. I recommend having some healthy snacks to consume periodically throughout the round. Fruit, energy bars, trail mix, and even peanut butter and jelly sandwiches are reasonable choices that will keep your energy levels (and your focus) consistent.

Water

Golfers are very susceptible to dehydration, especially on hot, sunny days. Don't rely on the golf course to provide water sources. Come prepared with your own H_2O, and keep drinking throughout the round.

Sun

Don't forget to protect yourself from the sun. Be sure to apply sunscreen before heading to the course (then wash your hands so your grip isn't slippery!). I would also recommend lip balm, a cap, and even UV-protective garments if you're extra sensitive to sunlight.

Eyewear

Wearing sunglasses while playing golf is not for everyone, but protecting your eyes from the sun, dust, and pollen makes sense. Even if you don't wear them while you swing, sunglasses are a good idea between shots!

playing opportunities

Golf is a sport that can be enjoyed in so many ways. As an individual, you can practice and work on your game, you can take lessons, or you can attend golf clinics. Golf also provides the opportunity to enjoy the thrills and challenges of the game on your own, without needing to arrange multiple schedules or find others to play with. Golf can also be a great escape—a sanctuary of sorts. Playing the game on your own can be a very relaxing experience. But there are so many more ways to play than as a single on your local course.

The social and fraternal aspects of golf are unmatched in other sports. As you become more comfortable with this game, it's likely that you will crave more opportunities to test your skills, play with other people, and "take your swing on the road." Well, I'm happy to deliver some great news—the possibilities are endless!

In this chapter, I will highlight and explore some of the many golf-related opportunities that exist. From tournament experiences and corporate events to unforgettable destinations, golf has so much to offer. You might start planning a buddy trip before you finish this book!

Public Course Opportunities

The first step should be a visit to your local public golf courses. Talk to the professional staff, browse the bulletin boards, and check for a facility website. Local courses offer group clinics, golf leagues, outing opportunities, and tournaments. I would strongly recommend joining a league in your area. Calling the public courses is the best way to get involved. Leagues can introduce you to a great group of fellow golfers; they also feature a variety of formats and help you perform under a different type of pressure. And if you and some friends want to start a league of your own, check out: www.golfleaguegenius.com.

Local Golf Associations

The United States is divided into 41 different PGA Sections. You should go to www.pga.com and find out which section you are in, and call their offices. They can bring you up to date on local tournament and golf event information, and put you in touch with other local golf associations (county, state, regional, and national). If you are in other parts of the world, the internet is usually your best bet for locating great sources of golf information and appropriate associations in your region.

Charity and Corporate Events

Many businesses host golf events for their employees and/or clients and potential clients—you might even work for one of those companies. If so, don't pass up the chance to tee it up at the company event. If not, you may be able to attend an event as a guest or a potential customer.

Charity golf events are also very popular. They are often held at private country clubs to raise money for a good cause. These events are sometimes a bit costly, but they enable you to play at a private facility that would otherwise be very difficult to access. Local papers, magazines, and websites can give you a list of these events, along with when and where they are taking place.

You might also call local clubs and see if there are any charity events that are looking for additional participants. Many of those events will feature an auction to raise additional funds. Other golf experiences are often offered as auction prizes. You can bid on (and hopefully win) the chance to play other courses—and feel good that your money is supporting the charity.

The PGA has divided the United States into 41 Sections, or regions. Like our Electoral College these regions are primarily defined by population density—for instance, the New England Section governs several states, while New York has four Sections dedicated to it alone. Each Section has its own board of directors and operates within the framework of the PGA Constitution; they also host their own tournaments and events, as well as apprentice and junior league programs. The Section websites are fonts of information—check them out to see what is happening in your area.

Alabama-Northwest Florida
https://alabamanwfloridapga.com/
(205) 621-6401

Northern California
https://ncpgalinks.com/
(707) 449-4742

Southern California
www.scpga.com
(951) 845-4653

Carolinas (North and South)
www.carolinas.pga.com
(336) 398-2742

Colorado
www.coloradopga.com
(303) 681-3992

Connecticut
www.ctpga.com
(860) 430-2302

North Florida
www.nfpga.com
(386) 256-1221

South Florida
www.sfpgagolf.com
(561) 729-0544

Gateway (Central Missouri, Southern Illinois)
www.gatewaypga.org
(636) 532-3355

Georgia
www.georgiapga.com
(678) 461-8600

Gulf States (Louisiana, Mississippi)
www.gspga.com
(504) 799-2444

Aloha (Hawaii)
www.aspga.com
(808) 593-2230

Illinois
www.ipga.com
(847) 729-5700

Indiana
www.indiagolf.org
(317) 738-9696

Iowa
www.iowapga.com
(319) 648-0026

Kentucky
www.kygolf.org
(502) 243-8295

Michigan
www.michiganpga.com
(517) 641-PGA1 (7421)

Middle Atlantic (District of Columbia, Maryland, Virginia)
www.mapga.com
(540) 720-7420

Midwest (Missouri, Kansas)
www.midwest.pga.com
(816) 229-6565

Minnesota
www.minnesotapga.com
(763) 754-0820

Nebraska
http://www.nebraskapga.com
(402) 489-7760

New England (Cape Cod, Maine, Massachusetts, New Hampshire, Rhode Island, Vermont)
www.nepga.com
(508) 869-0000

New Jersey
www.newjersey.pga.com
(732) 465-1212

Sun Country (New Mexico)
https://suncountrygolf.com/
(505) 897-0864

Central New York
www.cny.pga.com
(315) 446-5610

Metropolitan New York
www.met.pga.com
(914) 347-2325

Northeastern New York
www.neny.pga.com
(518) 438-8645

Western New York
www.westernnewyork.pga.com
(716) 626-7095

Northern Ohio
www.thenorthernohiopga.com
(216) 765-1214

Southern Ohio
www.thesouthernohiopga.com
(937) 754-4263

Pacific Northwest (Washington, Oregon, Western Montana)
www.pnwpga.com
(360) 456-6496

Philadelphia (Pennsylvania)
www.philadelphia.pga.com
(215) 886-7742

Rocky Mountain (Idaho, Eastern Montana, Northern Nevada, Ontario, Oregon, Wyoming)
www.rockymountainpga.com
(208) 939-6028

South Central (Arkansas, Oklahoma, Southern Kansas)
www.southcentral.pga.com
(918) 357-3332

Southwest (Arizona, Southern Nevada)
www.southwestpga.com
(480) 443-9002

Tennessee
https://tennpga.com/
(615) 790-7600

Northern Texas
www.ntpga.com
(214) 420-7421

Southern Texas
www.stpga.com
(832) 442-2404

Tri-State (Western Maryland, Western Pennsylvania, West Virginia)
www.tristate.pga.com
(724) 774-2224

Utah
www.utahpga.com
(801) 566-1005

Wisconsin
www.wisconsin.pga.com
(414) 443-3570

golf trips

Golf courses are some of the most beautiful pieces of property in the world, and offer golfers a great excuse to travel the globe (or even just your part of the world). Golf is frequently offered at some of the nicest destinations, and you should inquire about golf packages in the area you're planning to visit. Golf packages usually bundle options like accommodations, golf fees, meals, and pro shop merchandise together and arrive at a great price for the traveling golfer. Hopefully your family or business associates enjoy the game as much as you do, which would allow you to get a group discount.

Buddy Trips

Another option has become universally known as the "buddy trip." A golf buddy trip involves a group of friends who all love to golf at great courses. Since every member of the group shares the desire to play golf, a fun format for the trip can be planned. Daily tournaments can be arranged, different formats can be utilized, and usually you try to mix up the teams each day so you can play with as many different members of the group as possible. Travel agencies specialize in this form of travel, and you can always contact the destinations directly for trip details. For more information and assistance with organizing a memorable buddy trip, check out www.golftripgenius.com.

tournaments

Many beginning golfers cannot imagine signing up for a tournament. But tournaments should not intimidate you. As a beginner, you should seek events that use handicaps (a net division available). Team tournaments are also ideal for those new to the sport. Great examples would be:

An "A, B, C, D" tournament, where four golfers at different handicap levels join together on a team.

A "Scramble" tournament, which features a fairly forgiving and low-pressure format.

A "Pro-Am," where a PGA professional joins three amateur (nonprofessional) players to form a team. The Pro-Am is a great learning experience, since the pro in your group can help you with your swing and strategy as you compete.

Ultimately, you may get comfortable enough to enter tournaments that are more competitive. You should contact local golf clubs and associations for tournament opportunities and details. Most tournaments require that you have an official USGA handicap (find more information in Chapter 16). Make sure you get one!

Looking for a national or regional tournament—or just more information on golf events in your community? The best place to start is with your local golf association. There are more than 200 regional and state golf associations nationwide, including associations dedicated to women, juniors, and seniors. A great resource for finding all associations is the USGA website (https://www.usga.org/content/usga/home-page/about/find-your-allied-golf-association-usga-usa.html). Just click on the correct logo to find golf associations in your state. The USGA website is also a great source for everything from golf etiquette to handicapping, and even includes information on USGA-approved international golf associations.

insider lingo

I'm hopeful that you now have a greater understanding and appreciation for the great game of golf. The preceding chapters were designed to teach you the basics of the swing and give you the information necessary to head out into the world of golf and enjoy the sport! As you get more involved with the game, you'll find that there's a strong and very loyal population of golfers ... it's almost as if you're joining a huge club. Just making a practice swing in the hallway at your place of business could lead to countless golf conversations and even new friends.

You learned some basic terms in the opening chapter of this book, but this chapter gets a little less formal. Since I am now officially referring to you as a golfer, you should also know some of the insider lingo that can sound confusing, but is common verbiage in the golf community. These are the terms you're likely to hear in locker rooms, around water coolers, and from television golf commentators. I've listed some golf slang: words, phrases, and references that will help you join the golf conversation and fit right in. Don't feel the need to use this language too frequently, but enjoy being on "the inside" and being able to understand golf lingo.

ace   Another term for a hole-in-one; hitting your tee shot into the hole on a par 3.

airmail   If your approach shot sails long, and actually lands on the far side of the green, you "airmailed" the green.

albatross   Another term for the very rare double eagle, scoring a 2 on a par 5; a score of 3 under par on a single hole.

all square   A phrase in match play meaning the players are even or "tied"—no advantage to either side.

army golf   When a player keeps hitting the ball left, then right, left, right, etc., he is said to be playing "army" golf. He isn't hitting the ball straight.

back door   A term usually used when the golf ball curls into the cup from the far side after a big, breaking putt: "The ball fell in the back door."

banana ball   A term used for a big, dramatic slice.

beach   Another term for sand on the golf course, or a bunker.

big dog   The driver.

bite   A ball that spins a lot and holds the green has "bite."

bladed   A ball that is struck near the equator has been hit "thin" or "bladed."

breakfast ball   A do-over, usually on the first tee; also known as a mulligan. A fellow player may offer you to "take a breakfast ball," or have another try.

chili dip   A chip shot near the green that is poorly mis-hit. The club usually hits the ground and then bounces up into the middle of the ball, resulting in a poor shot.

choke   When a player who is nervous hits a bad shot, he has "choked" or not performed well under pressure.

chopper   A bad golfer.

chunked   A "chunked" shot takes place when the club hits the ground before the ball, and the ball barely moves forward.

cut   A cut is a controlled slice. A shot that spins the ball.

deck   The fairway. "He just hit a driver right off the deck."

dog track   A derogatory term for a golf course. If a course is poorly maintained and displeasing, it can be referred to as a "dog track."

dormie   In match play, when a player leads his opponent by the number of holes still remaining in the match. If you are winning by two holes and only two holes remain in the match, you are "dormie."

duck hook   A very dramatic hook. A low and violently spinning shot that curls far left of the target (for a right-hander).

duffer   A bad or struggling golfer.

flatstick   Another term for a putter.

flier   When a small amount of grass gets caught between the ball and the clubface at impact. The grass takes the spin off the shot, and the ball usually flies farther than normal and lands with virtually no spin. "That ball launched way over the green ... he must've caught a flier."

flop shot   A high-launching pitch shot with a very lofted club. The ball flies high and lands softly when you hit a nice flop shot.

flub   A poor shot—usually a "fat" shot.

foot wedge   Someone who cheats and kicks his ball out from behind a tree when nobody is looking is using a "foot wedge."

fried egg   When a ball plugs in the sand. A ball partially submerged in sand resembles a fried egg.

frog hair   The fringe or "apron" is short grass surrounding the putting surface—also known as frog hair.

gagged   "The player gagged" means that player choked, or did not perform well under pressure.

gimme   A ball that is so close to the hole there is no way you can miss.

goat track   Like "dog track," this term is used for a golf course that is disliked or in very poor condition.

hacker   A bad golfer.

hanging lie   When the ball is on higher ground in front of you, or above your feet, you have a hanging lie.

hardpan   Bare, compacted earth that no longer has turf.

hooded   A player who "hooded" his iron shot closed the clubface and hit a lower shot.

hosel rocket   Another term for "shank," when the ball is accidentally struck with the hosel or neck of the club.

hot   A ball that "comes out hot" has usually been hit out of rough. The ball is moving low, fast, and with very little spin.

idiot mark   A streak or mark on the crown of a driver or fairway wood. The mark comes from swinging under a ball on a tee. The ball leaves this mark on the top of the club.

inside the leather   A ball that's so close to the hole that if you were to stick the head of your putter in the cup and lay the club down on the green, the ball would be closer to the hole than the grip of the putter. Grips used to be made of leather; thus the ball is "inside the leather."

juice   A term for spin applied to a golf ball. "That ball had a lot of juice," so it held the green.

kick   Bounce. "The ball got a good kick and is now back in the fairway."

knee-knocker   A relatively short putt, but just long enough to make a player nervous.

knockdown shot   A lower-trajectory shot, usually used to flight a golf ball low and under the wind.

lag   **1.** A safe, defensive putt from a long distance: "Rather than attack, the player lagged the ball close to the hole." **2.** The angle between the left forearm and the clubshaft during the downswing.

lay-up   A shot that is not intended to reach the green. It's a safer shot that is designed to position a player nicely for the next shot.

lift, clean, and place   When a match is being played in very wet conditions, the tournament director will sometimes allow golfers to play "lift, clean, and place," which means you can mark the position of your ball in play, pick it up, clean it, and place it back on the ground on a spot no closer to the hole than the original position—without incurring a penalty.

lip   The edge of a bunker, and also the round edge of the hole.

lip-out   When a ball nearly goes in the hole, but catches the edge and spins out without finding the bottom of the cup.

looper   A caddie who finishes a round of golf for his player just completed a "loop." "Looper" is another term for caddie.

mulligan   Another term for a "do-over," or a second try. There's no mention of mulligan in the rules of golf, but many players like to give each other another chance after a bad shot. (A mulligan does not conform with the official rules of golf.)

nip it   A phrase meaning to strike a ball cleanly and crisply without taking a divot.

O.B.   Out of bounds.

over-the-top   When a player approaches the ball from above the ideal swing path. The club swings "over" the ball, and catches the outside of it, generally leading to poor results.

pin high   When a player hits an approach shot that was the perfect distance (even though it may be left or right of the flag), it's even with the flag, or pin high.

preferred lies   Just like "lift, clean, and place," this is sometimes allowed by a tournament committee when conditions are particularly wet or bad.

punch shot   Usually just a half or three-quarter swing, the punch is a low, driving shot that is used to escape trouble, or to keep the ball low and under the wind.

re-load   Usually used after hitting a ball out of play; the player may say "I better re-load," and hit another ball.

ready golf   When a group decides not to wait for the player farthest from the hole to play first. Ready golf simply means there's no need to wait for the proper order of play. Whoever is ready to hit can go ahead and swing.

sandbagger   A sandbagger is a golfer who intentionally keeps a high handicap, but then plays better when needed. Golfers frown on sandbagging.

shank   A shot that results from the ball being struck by the hosel or neck of the club.

shoot your age   One of the ultimate goals in golf is to someday shoot your age, meaning your score for 18 holes matches (or is lower than) your age.

short grass   Another term for the fairway.

short-sided   If an approach shot misses the green to the right, and the flag is located in the right side of that green, the player has not left much room to recover. Missing on the same side as the pin is called short-siding yourself.

shotgun   A shotgun start means that multiple groups of golfers all start at the same time, but on different holes.

shrimp   The shrimp is a dramatic, violent hook. The flight of the ball curves sharply and is similar in shape to a shrimp.

sit   A command. If a ball is struck, and the player feels it is probably going to go too far, he may yell "Sit!" hoping that the ball stops quickly.

skulled   A ball that was hit "thin" or near the equator was "skulled."

snap hook   The snap hook is a frustrating shot. For a right-handed player, the ball leaves the clubface on a relatively low trajectory, then curves sharply to the left.

snowman   An 8 on the scorecard.

stinger   A powerful shot with low, piercing trajectory. This shot was made famous by Tiger Woods.

tap-in   A putt of a very short distance. The ball is so close to the hole, all you have to do is tap it in.

Texas wedge   A name for a putter when used beyond the putting surface, off the green.

the 19th hole   Another term for the clubhouse, and specifically the bar at the clubhouse.

the tips   Another term for the most challenging set of tees at a golf course. To play a course at its maximum length is playing "from the tips."

three-jack   Another term for a three-putt, or needing three putts to get your ball in the cup on a given green.

tight lie   When there is very little turf under your ball, or the grass under your ball is very closely mown, you have a tight lie.

toe shank   While the shank is a shot that contacts the hosel, a toe shank occurs when the ball is just barely struck by the toe of the club. The ball will sail directly to the right (for a right-handed player).

turkey   When you birdie three straight holes, you've made a turkey.

up and down   When you hit your ball onto the green, then hole the very next putt, you've completed an up and down.

vanity handicap   The opposite of the sandbagger, a person with a vanity handicap is not as good as his handicap indicates. This person only likes to enter good scores, and takes more pride in his handicap than in his true ability.

waggle   Part of a pre-swing routine where a player relieves tension by moving the club back and forth a bit before committing to the backswing.

winter rules   Another term for "preferred lies." Winter rules refers to a form of golf where abnormal course conditions call for the lift, clean, and place allowances.

yips   A condition in which unintended twitching of the hand muscles occurs. Primarily seen during the putting stroke, the yips make it very difficult to swing the putter head accurately.

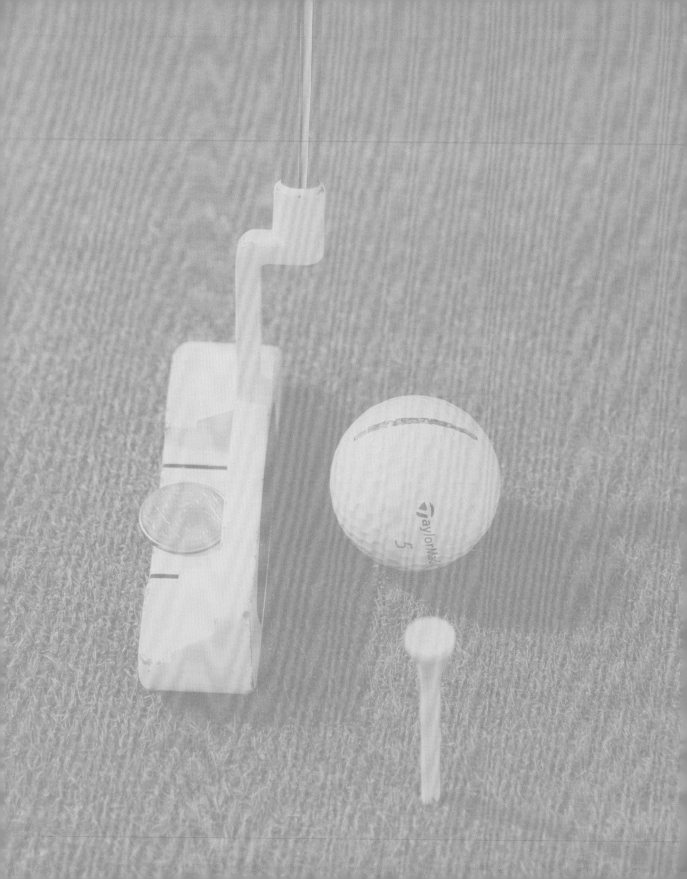

practice Drills

In golf, as in life, practice makes perfect. As you begin to play the game more regularly, you may notice that there are areas that require a little extra attention. The Drills in this section will allow you to address any of those issues or weaknesses and help you to take that next step in your game. There are Drills here for putting, chipping, bunker play, and even the full swing. Of course, no two swings are alike, and every golfer is different, so I don't expect every Drill to be perfect for you. Experiment, have fun, and see which of these Drills help your game the most.

Drill 1: Alignment on the Green

I've mentioned how important proper alignment is for your full swing—and proper alignment is equally critical when putting! If you're missing too many short putts to the right or the left (or both), this alignment Drill will help you set up properly, and hole more putts on the course.

1. Find a fairly level area of the practice putting green.

2. Set up the alignment station as shown. Allow enough room to the inside of the far alignment rod for the toe of the putter to pass freely, and add a little extra room for the heel side (since the putter may "arc" to the inside a bit during the backswing and follow-through).

3. Address the ball. This station will help you position your feet parallel to the desired target line. It will also show you whether your putter face is set up squarely.

4. Practice making putts of 3 or 4 feet (1 to 1.5m) from this station.

WHAT YOU WILL NEED

Putter

Ball

Two straight sticks, approximately 48'' (122cm) long; 2 long irons from your golf bag would also do the trick.

The face should be at a perfect 90-degree angle relative to the alignment rods.

Drill 2: Strike a Line

If you're lacking confidence on those short, simple putts, this Drill can help. The chalk line will not only help square your putter, it will also help you chart the movement of your putter throughout the stroke. Although it's important to keep your gaze on the ball until after impact, this Drill seems to help golfers "see" the line of their short putts much better.

1. Find a level area of the practice green.

2. Insert the tee into the grass behind the hole. Secure one end of the string on the tee.

3. Reel out 6 or 7 feet (2 to 2.5m) of the chalk line.

4. Holding the reel side of the line steady, pick up the middle of the string, and let it snap back to the turf to create a chalk line.

5. Place your ball on the center of the chalk line.

6. Address the ball. You'll instantly be able to tell if the face of your putter is square (perpendicular) to your target.

Drill 3: Wrist Stabilizer

One of the most common flaws in putting is excessive hinging or flipping of the wrists. That extra (and totally unnecessary) motion makes it difficult to strike the ball with the center of the putter face, and missing the "sweet spot" makes it impossible to control distance. This Drill forces your wrists to stay firm and stable throughout the stroke, leading to better contact and lower scores.

WHAT YOU WILL NEED

Ball

Putter

1. Place a ball between the end of the putter grip and the inside of your right forearm as shown.

2. Take a few practice strokes and feel the sensation of "quiet" wrists. No hinging or unhinging should take place. Both the left and right wrist are essentially locked in position throughout the stroke. To keep the ball in place, you need to make a smooth rocking motion with your shoulders, and limit the movements of your hands and wrists—a recipe for excellent putting.

Athletes in every sport know the importance of breathing properly. It's common to see professional basketball players exhale just before attempting a critical free throw. The exhale relaxes the nerves and allows for an easy, comfortable motion. Try that same theory with putting. Exhale just before you begin your stroke—it's likely to relax you and lead to a smoother stroke.

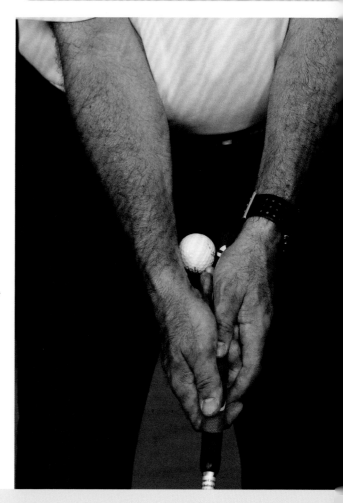

Drill 4: the Tee Gate

If the putter head is zigging and zagging throughout your stroke, scores are likely to rise. A consistent path back and through the ball will lead to great success on the greens. This simple Drill of creating a "gate" with tees will force you to focus on the path of your putter and help you to find the "sweet spot" or center of the putter face more often.

1. Set your putter head behind the ball.

2. Insert one tee in the ground about .5 inch (1.5cm) beyond the toe, and insert the other tee .5 inch inside the heel.

3. Take a practice swing. If you zig or zag the putter, you'll get instant feedback in the form of hitting a tee. Keep positioning balls into the starting position and swinging your putter successfully through the gate.

WHAT YOU WILL NEED

Putter

Ball

Two tees

Practice green

Drill 5: Putting Under the String

One of the most common flaws in putting is excessive hinging or flipping of the wrists. That extra (and totally unnecessary) motion makes it difficult to strike the ball with the center of the putter face, and missing the "sweet spot" makes it impossible to control distance. This Drill forces your wrists to stay firm and stable throughout the stroke, leading to better contact and lower scores.

WHAT YOU WILL NEED

Two pencils

String

Ball

Putter

Practice green

1. Find a level stretch of practice green and stick one pencil in the green a few inches behind the hole. Stick the other pencil in the green 4 or 5 feet (1 to 1.5m) in front of the hole. Attach the string from the top of one pencil to the top of the other.

2. Place a ball directly under the string and take your address position. At this point, you can check two key positions:

   a. If the face of your putter is perpendicular to the string, that means it's nice and square to the target line.

   b. If the ball is perfectly bisected by the string, that means your eyes are positioned directly above the ball, which is ideal.

3. Your putting motion can also benefit from this setup. As you make a stroke from this position, the hovering string will encourage you to keep the putter low and fairly level with the ground, which leads to better contact.

Drill 6: The One-Handed Putt

If you tend to jab at the ball, or have trouble finding the proper speed on the greens, this Drill is for you. Putting with one hand can help you find a good rhythm and tempo; it also forces you to pay close attention to the path of your putter throughout the stroke. Nice tempo and a consistent path will lead to lower scores!

1. Grasp the putter with just your right hand. Keeping the left hand off the club, make a few comfortable putts. You'll notice that the club feels a bit heavier, and that you have to be more relaxed and patient with your movements to make it swing consistently.

2. Switch and try a few putts with just your left hand holding the club.

3. Now putt using both hands, and try to maintain that same comfortable rhythm.

If you need something to keep your other hand busy, try holding a couple of golf balls.

Drill 7: Tennis, Anyone?

Technique is important, but confidence is critical—especially when it comes to putting. Uncertainty leads to a tentative motion, which leads to missed putts ... even from short range. Believe it or not, tennis can actually help your golf game. You may think I'm crazy, but if you want to build confidence on the putting green, this Drill can really help.

WHAT YOU WILL NEED

Tennis balls

Putter

Practice green

1. Position yourself 2 or 3 feet (.5 to 1m) from the cup. Place the tennis ball as you would a golf ball.

2. Make a normal putting stroke, rolling the tennis ball toward the hole. The tennis ball is nearly the size of the opening, so it's difficult to make these putts—but keep trying.

3. Once you sink a few tennis balls, switch to a regular golf ball. It's like rolling a marble into a garbage can—you won't believe how easy it seems!

Drill 8: Rubber Bands

If you want to make more putts, you need to find the sweet spot, or the center of your putter face. A ball that is struck squarely in the center of the putter face is more likely to roll true and find the bottom of the cup.

1. Wrap the rubber bands around your putter head on either side of the sweet spot, leaving approximately 1 inch (2.5cm) between the bands.

2. Set down your ball. Address the ball and make a stroke. If you hit the ball in the center of the putter face, it will feel clean and solid and roll forward nicely. If you miss, the ball will make contact with a rubber band and bounce dramatically to the left or right, and the sound of impact will be muffled.

These tips can make a huge difference in your game, but equipment can also influence results. If you struggle with a shaky putting stroke, you can try a number of different ways to hold the putter (as outlined in Chapter 7). You might also consider changing the actual grip on your putter. There are oversized (thicker) putter grips that can be purchased and installed to help limit hand and wrist motion during the stroke. See your local PGA professional for details.

Drill 9: Coin Drop

Great putters have a smooth tempo and rhythm to their stroke. Some golfers have a nice takeaway, but change directions too quickly and jab at the ball with their putting stroke. That jab makes it very difficult to judge speed. This coin Drill can help you develop a nice rhythm on the greens.

WHAT YOU WILL NEED

Quarter

Tee

Ball

Putter with a cavity

1. Stick a tee in the ground and place a ball in front of it, even with the tee. Position a quarter in the cavity of the putter.

2. Make your normal stroke. If you have good tempo, the quarter will stay in the cavity until the moment when the putter meets the ball. The impact will then force the quarter out of the cavity, dropping it evenly with the tee.

3. If you take the putter back and change directions too quickly, the coin will drop out of the cavity long before the putter reaches the ball. Keep practicing until you drop the coin next to the tee every time.

Drill 10: One-Handed Chipping

One of the biggest problems in chipping is overuse of the hands and wrists. When they become too active, the motion looks jumpy and out of sync. Much like one-handed putting, this Drill helps to quiet the hands and develop more feel for the chipping motion.

1. Grasp the club with just your right hand. Keeping the left hand at your side, try a few swings to loosen up and develop better tempo. Feel the weight of the club, and how your swing becomes more patient and smooth.

2. Once you're comfortable with the one-handed swing, introduce a ball and hit a bunch of one-handed chips.

3. When you've mastered the one-handed chip, put both hands back on the club and see if you can continue to feel the club swinging comfortably. If not, go back to using just one hand. Soon you'll find a better rhythm.

Allow the weight of the club to create a natural hinge during the backswing. As you swing down through impact, you need to keep your right arm moving smoothly to the finish. This smooth arm motion leads to better contact. If you were to stop your arm, your wrists would unhinge too dramatically, leading to poor contact and inconsistent results.

WHAT YOU WILL NEED

Iron

Ball

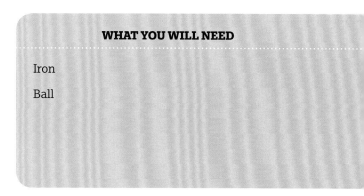

Drill 11: Chipping with Two Clubs

"Flipping" or unhinging the wrists through impact is a common flaw in chipping. When you get too wristy with these delicate little shots, it's impossible to make clean and consistent contact with the ball. The two-club Drill addresses that very issue, and forces your wrists to stay firm through the shot.

WHAT YOU WILL NEED

Two irons

Ball

1. Select a club and set up for a normal chip shot. Then take your second iron and grasp it down by the clubhead so that the original club is leaning toward the target in a proper chipping setup, and the second shaft is positioned under your left arm and up along your side.

2. Holding the two clubs, make a few practice chipping swings. If your wrists stay firm and your body rotates properly, the extended shaft should stay to the left of your body as shown in the photo. If you flip those wrists through impact, the extended shaft will hit you in the rib cage—instant feedback! Keep practicing until you can comfortably chip without feeling contact from the extended shaft.

Drill 12: The Clipboard

Many golfers struggle with their bunker shots. A common mistake is to dig too deeply into the sand, leading to an absence of follow-through. The clipboard Drill can help you feel the acceleration through to the finish position, and give you confidence when you're in the sand!

1. Place a clipboard into the sand with the clip facing down, sprinkle some sand in the middle of the board, and place a ball on top.

2. Address the ball as if it were an ordinary bunker shot. The key here is to take just a small swing. Your sand wedge should strike the board and skid smoothly to the finish. The board encourages a shallower pass through the sand, and also speeds the club through the ball to a better finish.

Use caution on this Drill. Swing at a slower speed and make sure to contact the board 1 or 2 inches (2.5 to 5cm) before the ball. If you swing down too steeply, you could catch the front edge of the board and damage your club.

Drill 13: Feet Together

A common problem in the full swing is swaying or sliding–in other words, too much lateral movement. If you move around too much during your swing, this Drill can be very helpful in making a more stable and centered swing.

1. Begin in your normal full swing address position, and then bring your feet together.

2. Take a few small practice swings without moving your feet. These are not full swings, just halfway back and halfway through. You will begin to feel your body turning naturally and staying more centered. If you were to sway or slide out of position, you would fall!

3. After a few small practice swings, hit a few balls off a tee with the same small swing while keeping your feet together.

Drill 14: Slapshot

Golfers who slice the ball, or tend to miss all their shots to the right, may have tightness in the hands and forearms. That tightness limits the rotation of the clubface through impact. This Drill will force you to feel exaggerated rotation of both the forearms and the clubface.

1. Grab an iron and take your normal address position.

2. Keep your left hand on the grip in its normal place, but slide your right hand all the way down below the grip and position it on the shaft of the club.

3. Take a few small practice swings. This "split grip" will give you a strong sense of rotation, and the clubface will close rapidly through the impact area. Keep the swings small, and don't hit balls with this Drill.

4. After you get the hang of the rotation, return to a normal grip, but keep that split-grip sensation as you swing. Say goodbye to the slice!

WHAT YOU WILL NEED

Iron

Ball

Drill 15: The Chair

Earlier in this book you learned the importance of maintaining your spine tilt through impact. Well, that can be easier said than done. Many golfers have a tendency to stand up, or lose their spine angle at the top of the backswing or at impact. The chair drill will help you maintain the proper spine tilt and develop a centered and consistent swing.

1. Place a chair behind you, with the back of the chair facing you.

2. Take your normal address position with, or without a club (as shown). After finding proper posture, slowly back up against a chair so that the back pockets of your pants are just touching it.

3. Make a few relaxed practice swings, trying to maintain contact with the chair throughout the motion—even as your hips rotate naturally.

At the top of the backswing, your back right pocket should be touching the chair.

At impact, your back left pocket should now be touching the chair.

If you complete the entire motion correctly, your left hip should be touching the chair.

Drill 16: The Wall

Many golfers have difficulty maintaining a good, stable axis. A very common example of this is leaning forward during the swing. When a golfer's head moves forward significantly, it can lead to poor contact and even the "shanks"—where the hosel of the club strikes the ball. The wall drill will cure the shanks and help you hit better shots more consistently.

1. Simply take your address posture without using a club and position yourself so that your head is 1 inch (2.5cm) from a wall.

2. Take a backswing. If your head hits the wall, you'll know your head is moving forward. Keep practicing and make sure you stay away from the wall on the way back and at impact.

WHAT YOU WILL NEED

Wall